Making the Connections

Women, Work, and Abuse

Making the Connections

Women, Work, and Abuse

Patricia A. Murphy, Ph.D.

PERMISSION TO REPRINT the "Diagnostic Criteria for 309.89 Post-
traumatic Stress Disorder," from *Diagnostic and Statistical Manual of
Mental Disorders, Third Edition, Revised,* Washington, DC, 1987, was
granted by the American Psychiatric Association. G. Michael Graham's
Areas of Expertise for Vocational Experts was adapted from his seminar
materials with his permission. The National Association of Rehabilitation
Professionals in the Private Sector (NARPPS) agreed to the reprinting of
their "Primary Care Vocational Standards," from the *NARPPS 1989/1990
National Directory of Rehabilitation Professionals, Vocational/Medical
Facilities, Products and Services.*

ISBN: 1-878205-65-X
Library of Congress Catalog Card Number: 92-075487
Printed in the United States of America

about the photo

Maiden, mother, and crone; the three phases of a woman's life all compressed into the girl child. The broom as the symbol of the crone/witch. A tool obviously too large for her and yet the culture of the fathers expects her to use it anyway. The pinafore/apron as the symbol of the mother who nurtures, cleans, cooks, and brings children into the world of the fathers. The pinafore/apron is no protection from the male imperative to impregnate her, to sexualize her. The owl-eye glasses as the virgin goddess/maiden symbol. She sees all. She calls upon the wise child within.

The year is 1950, and she is of that generation of women who are the very foundation of the Quiet Revolution. She stands on the threshold between home and world. She is of the generation caught between two worlds of work, one waged and one not.

Photograph courtesy of a generous co-researcher.

dedication

For Lee Stone

contents

confidentiality

All the stories in this book are true. Names, locations, occupations, race, ages, abuse experience(s), and other identifying details have been altered to protect the privacy of the co-researchers. Workers' compensation case stories have undergone similar alteration. Readers who find their stories in this book do so because they are not alone. Unhappily, the abuse stories in this book are not unique.

acknowledgments

My thanks to Lee Stone who sparked the writing of
this book; to Jane Caputi, Loretta Birckhead, Faramarz
Nateghian, Maureen Peer Oliver, Michael Graham, Kathy
Kauffman, and Penny MacElveen-Hoehn for being there
as I struggled; to Nancy Hamel and May Tsushima of
Sojourn Services For Formerly Battered Women and
Their Children in Santa Monica, California, for letting me
try out ideas with them, and to Carol Arnett, also of
Sojourn, who helped me launch a national pro bono
movement; to all the co-researchers for the courageous
sharing of their stories; to Jeanne Simonoff, my writing
partner and patient listener; to Patti Bengtson, my business partner and number-crunching consultant; to
Colleen Davids Flippo for her editing skills; and to Minnie
Bruce Pratt for so kindly stepping in at the end.

And particularly, to Caroline Shrodes. I miss the
clarity of you more and more as each day passes without
you.

author's note

This book is arranged so that stories appear in front of each of the 11 chapters. There are two reasons for this arrangement. The first is to give the eight co-researchers, who had the courage to explore with me how the abuse in their lives had forever changed their identities as workers, their own words, and the right to tell their stories in their own way. (Three of the stories are told by me because these survivors of abuse and vocational dysfunction could not raise their own voices, their own words, and I cannot forget them or their stories.)

Secondly, this is the way we work, rehabilitationists and anti-abuse worker's alike. The story comes first. Then the counseling hypothesis, the evaluation, the business of connecting the fragile breathing human to the arcane and dead rules of welfare systems, rehabilitation systems, medical/legal systems.

introduction

In 1984, an old friend of mine, Lee Stone, asked me to assist her in maintaining the California Federation of Business and Professional Women USA's legislative plank on violence against women. In her capacity as the state legislation chair, she had become aware of members within the organization who wished to remove the violence against women plank because *they did not perceive violence against women as a business or professional issue.*

In my work as a vocational rehabilitation counselor providing services to industrially injured workers in the California workers' compensation system, I had become aware of how violence against women was not only an on-the-job injury for some women but was also present in women's lives outside of their jobs. The combination of an industrial injury and an abuse history outside the job was devastating for many women in my case load.

My friend understood I would be passionately incensed by any notion that abuse against women has nothing to do with their work lives. Consequently, I addressed the California Federation of Business and Professional Women USA members at their Government in Action Conference in Sacramento, California on February 25, 1984.

The California Federation (1990, July) did maintain their plank on abuse issues, and the legislative platform for 1990-1991 includes the following: "Ensure equitable family laws, assist the victims of and prevent all forms of violence, assault and abuse."

My speech (Murphy, 1988a), *Abuse: A Blight On Our Success,* was published in an anthology on child abuse. I then wrote and published two novels on abuse issues (Murphy, 1987, 1988b). I told myself that somebody would develop the ideas presented in Sacramento into a book. I didn't think it would be me. I wanted to write novels. But after a decade of providing vocational rehabilitation services to more than 500 industrially injured workers in the California workers' compensation system, I discovered that I did not want to give up my profession and the mythical somebody had never done that book. *Somebody* has turned out to be me.

the quiet revolution

Between the years 1986 and 2000, the number of women in the U.S. labor force will increase from 52 million to 66 million. Women's rate of participation in the labor force is twice that of men. By the year 2000, women will constitute 47% of the labor force (Harlan & Steinberg, 1989).

This phenomenal movement of women from the private life of the home and family into the public life of waged work has occurred within three decades (Matthaei, 1982). At 20, I was in the minority as a fully employed female worker, but at 50 I am in the majority. My housewife sister now complains to me of being misunderstood and unappreciated. We have traded minority and majority status.

Journal articles lament the lack of a complete career psychology for women, but scholarship on women's work appears to be restricted to research on women's vocational choices and their impact on the family (Fitzgerald & Crites, 1980; Ibrahim & Herr, 1987). This is, of course, critical research because women are still the primary caretakers of the family despite their additional responsibilities in the waged work world (Wages For Housework, 1990; Waring, 1988).

However, feminist scholars point to a lack of sophistication in feminist theories of women in the workforce and pose a challenging list of questions for women's studies educators to consider (Brandi, 1990):

> What does equality of employment mean for women and men? What do participation and equality mean under the law in light of growing income differentials? What does it mean for employees who lack control of fertility, individual autonomy, and access to employment? What is the role of women's studies in relation to

women's work, if the largest numbers of women are economically
marginalized as women's studies becomes increasingly
professionalized? (p. 8)

And although the issues of individual autonomy and
access to employment are directly related to violence against
women, nowhere is the issue of violence against women
addressed. One of the central questions of this book is: *How
can there ever be a complete career psychology of women or
sophisticated feminist theory about women's work without
taking into account violence against women in their waged
and unwaged work lives?*

the lesson of the montreal massacre

On December 6, 1989, Marc Lepine, a 25-year-old unemployed Canadian, invaded a classroom at the University
of Montreal's School of Engineering. He separated the men
from the women and then shot the women at close range
with a .223-caliber Sturm Ruger, a semiautomatic sport
weapon. Fourteen women died; nine women and four men
were wounded. Marc Lepine's rage was directed against
women, particularly against women he identified as "feminists." The women in the classroom were apparently "feminists" because they were enrolled in an engineering class
and supposedly expected not only to work, but to work in
this nontraditional career for women. Lepine killed himself
after the massacre leaving behind a suicide note documenting his hatred of "feminists" (Pitt, 1989a, b).

It would be comforting to dismiss Lepine's woman-
hating rampage as an isolated event, the actions of a mad-
man. Unfortunately, this is not a luxury open to women.
Feminist thinkers have had to develop new language for
what Dworkin (1976) describes as "...the systematic crip-
pling, raping and/or killing of women by men.... We must
finally understand that under patriarchy *gynocide* is the
ongoing reality of life lived by women" (p. 19).

Femicide is the term used by the Clearinghouse on
Femicide, described by its coordinator, Chris Domingo
(1990), as "the first non-profit organization in the world
doing study, research, and consciousness-raising on the

problem of misogynist murder as it occurs in the United States and throughout the world" (p. 1).

Caputi (1987) asserts that "we live in the midst of a period of intensified gynocide, equivalent in destruction to the European Witchcraze and recorded, if not in the inadequate or unavailable statistics, in the widespread embedding of sex crime and its ideology into legend, fiction, film, fashion, and most of all, pornography" (p. 96).

Caputi's (1987) concepts raise two important issues. The first is the notion of sex crime as embedded into the culture and therefore also into the workplace. Recognition of this reality is now codified into employment law in the phrase *hostile work environment*. The stuff of workplace harassment is derived from the ideology of sex crime in the pornographic calendars on the walls, the obscene remarks, the sexual assaults. A hostile work environment has been described (Bornn, 1990) as one in which:

> Conduct occurs (whether verbal, physical or visual) and sufficiently offends, humiliates, distresses or intrudes upon its intended victim, that it disrupts her emotional tranquility in the workplace (e.g., it weighs heavily on her mind, spirits, or senses), affects her ability to perform her job as usual (e.g., it causes her to feel fatigued, overwhelmed, or distressed), or otherwise interferes with and undermines her personal sense of well being (e.g., she feels that the workplace has become unfriendly or antagonistic toward her). (pp. 3-4)

Both federal and state employment laws also recognize "nondirect harassment" which is defined as being forced to "work in an atmosphere in which such harassment was severe and pervasive" (Bornn, 1990, p. 4).

The Montreal massacre is an example of both direct and nondirect harassment of women and constitutes an extreme example of the concept of the hostile work environment. A good example of a mild version of the hostile work environment is the failure of the University of California at Santa Barbara to include bathrooms for women when the engineering classroom building was constructed. In fact, one of the underground justifications for the creation of the campus women's center was the stories among campus clerical workers about secretaries from the engineering building wandering the campus to find a bathroom they could call their own.

As we shall see, it would be difficult to locate a work environment for women which is not hostile and which is free of both direct and nondirect harassment. This is because women's work takes place both in the private sphere (unwaged work in the home and family) and in the public sphere (waged work in the open labor market). Therefore, the lesson of the Montreal massacre is that the ideology of sex crime is not only embedded into legend, fiction, film, fashion, and pornography, but also into the educational arena and its extension, the workplace.

The second issue Caputi's (1987) comments raise is the problem of reliable statistics. The estimates of women killed in the witch-burning centuries in Europe range from 200,000 to nine million and the same extremes are represented in today's statistics.

Anderson and McMaken (1990) note that various research indicates rates of sexual abuse ranging from 6% to 62% for females and 3% to 31% for males. The lack of systematic data collection on local, state, and national levels is lamentable.

Russell's (1986) scientifically sound, large-scale study of the sexual abuse of girls offers firmer ground. Nineteen percent of the 930 women surveyed reported at least one experience of incestuous abuse and 16% of those had experienced abuse before the age of 18.

Research figures (Schmidt, Crimando, & Riggar, 1990) for sexual harassment in the workplace range from 42% to 90% of women and 3% to 15% of men, based on various studies which used different methodologies. Between 85% and 90% for women and around 5% for men are now considered accurate.

Rape statistics also reveal widely varying estimates. Russell (1984) found her estimate of nonmarital rapes of females at a rate 13 times higher than the total rape rate reported by the Uniform Crimes Reports for 1972 in San Francisco. Russell's study indicated that when attempted and completed nonmarital rapes are combined, 41% of the women surveyed had suffered this experience. Exclusion of attempted nonmarital rapes leaves the figure at 31%.

Marital rape is still NOT a crime in Missouri, New Mexico, North Carolina, Oklahoma, South Carolina, and Utah. Given the lack of consistency in data collection and the recent history of marital rape as a crime, valid statistics are difficult to come by. The submerging of marital rape into wife battering may conceal the level of the problem. However, estimates by Russell (1990b) place marital rape rates at one in seven women who have ever been married.

Some researchers (Gelles & Straus, 1988) estimate wife battering rates between 21% and 34%. This means over one and one-half million women in the United States are physically assaulted by a partner each year. Some feminists (Dworkin, 1989) now put the figure closer to 50%.

And if these figures aren't challenging and provocative enough, other data (Anderson & McMaken, 1990) show an escalation in violence against women and children while some researchers find violence declining. A 55% increase in known child abuse cases between 1980 and 1985 was reported by the U.S. House of Representatives Select Committee on Children, Youth, and Families (Anderson & McMaken, 1990). In comparison, Gelles and Straus' (1988) research shows a decline in child abuse with one and one-half million children still being abused each year.

Russell's (1984) San Francisco study of 930 adult women indicates that the rape rate is rising. She writes: "These data predict that the rates for women currently in their teens and 20s will eventually be higher. By age 20 the percentage reporting one or more completed or attempted rapes has increased steadily from 11% of women 60 and older to almost 30% of the youngest group" (pp. 36-37).

The Gelles and Straus (1988) telephone survey of 6,002 homes indicates a decline in wife battering from 1975 to 1985 but still leaves an estimated one and one-half million women being assaulted each year.

Most available statistical data on abuse do not include data on women identified as prostitutes, but perhaps no single group of women experiences more violence than prostitutes. Since its founding in 1984, The Council for

Prostitution Alternatives (CPA) in Portland, Oregon has assembled the following data based on information obtained from more than 800 prostitution survivors using CPA's services (Neland, undated):

♦ 27 have disappeared and are presumed murdered since 1984 (in the Portland, Oregon area)
♦ 80% are victims of rape; 8 to 10 times per year
♦ 83% are victims of aggravated assaults
♦ 57% are victims of kidnap
♦ 85% suffer from drug and alcohol addiction
♦ 57% have seriously attempted suicide
♦ 70% are victims of incest. (p. iii)

The concept of prostitution as violence against women is a slowly surfacing notion which must rise against deeply ingrained prejudices. Understanding prostitution as violence against women will require nothing less than a paradigm shift. Until that occurs, all statistical data on abuse are suspect since they exclude this large class of women (estimated at one million women engaged in prostitution in the United States at any given time) (WHISPER, 1990).

women's work

I am reduced to mental sputtering and stuttering when I try to write about women's work. It's like falling into a vast bowl of semantic and political spaghetti. I slip and slide no matter which way I turn, but one thing has become clear. Just as prostitution cannot be left out of any discussion of violence against women, it cannot be left out of any discussion of women's work. This is not because I accept any construction of prostitution as work, but because as Giobbe (1990) states, "Prostitution is a form of exploitation that is paradigmatic of women's social, sexual, and economic subordination under patriarchy" (p. 4).

In 1973, the charismatic Margo St. James founded COYOTE (Call Off Your Old Tired Ethics) in San Francisco. St. James defined prostitution as lucrative work for women. And although the National Organization for Women and other mainstream feminist and liberal groups (e.g., the American Civil Liberties Union) accepted prostitution as work and encouraged decriminalization, ideological differences surfaced immediately (Hobson, 1987).

These differences continue and have not been resolved by feminist activists. The passage of two resolutions at the 12th Annual Conference of the National Coalition Against Sexual Assault (July, 1990a, b) in Denver, Colorado in July 1990 is a good example. One resolution is titled, "Support For Sex Trade Workers" and calls for the decriminalization of prostitution and notes that "for many women and children the only alternative to prostitution is starvation." The resolution lists social services which should be available to prostitutes (e.g., shelters, detoxification centers and programs) and urges support for women who wish to remain in the sex industry.

Another resolution urges the National Coalition Against Sexual Assault to recognize prostitution as violence against women. This resolution also supports the provision of services to prostitutes. The issue of decriminalization is negated in favor of abolishing all laws penalizing women and children, but demands both enforcement and an increase in penalties against those who use and profit from the prostitution of women and children.

So is prostitution work or isn't it? And what is work anyway? There are notions of work as punishment or as religious duty, as productive activity for others, as family work (e.g., child care and housework), and as activities which people do as part of their own fulfillment (Gerstel & Gross, 1987).

Glazer (1987) writes that in a capitalist economy, we define work as "those activities which produce goods and/or services and/or provide for the circulation of goods and services which are directly or indirectly for capitalism" (p. 236).

Prostitution certainly meets Glazer's (1987) definition of work under capitalism in that it is an activity which provides a service directly or indirectly for capitalism or the accumulation of money. Slavery also meets Glazer's definition, and prostitution has been defined as *female sexual slavery* (Barry, 1979). I do not accept prostitution as work. I define it both as slavery and as violence against women.

However, the power of the patriarchy is such that the control of definitions of work for women is open to manipulation in order to service its needs or whims. As we shall see, this holds true for prostitution or housework and child care or the provision of sexual services within a marriage.

For example, in the state of Nevada, prostitution is work if it's done in Storey, Nye, Lincoln, or Esmeralda Counties. If the same activities take place in Reno, Las Vegas, Incline Village, or anywhere else in the United States, it's a crime. And even within the legal boundaries in the state of Nevada, prostitutes are expected to respond to both written and unwritten rules of doubtful legal validity. These laws are formulated and enforced randomly at the whim of local law officials (Symanski, 1974).

This appears to be a pattern in the sex industry, as explained by Mary Johnson (1987), former president of the Canadian Association of Burlesque Entertainers (CABE). The Canadian attorney general sometimes enforced the criminal code against nude dancing and sometimes he didn't. This meant that the dancers never knew if they were working or committing a crime.

Similar machinations occur with housewives. Although the work of housewives and mothers is not considered a crime, housewives and mothers are also punished by legal systems in the manipulation of their status as workers. In 1978, the Supreme Court of the state of California determined a policy that all "supported spouses" should seek employment and work toward becoming self-supporting (Sherman, 1990). This means that the marriage contract has now become an arrangement where women's work as mothers and housewives is recognized at the beginning of the marriage and then invalidated at the end of the marriage (generally after the woman has lost her youthful sex-object status) when the man decides to move on. The woman's work is then "disappeared" and she is expected to become "employed." The author of California's no-fault divorce law, James Hayes, expected his wife of 33 years to go to "work" even though she suffers from severe arthritis and asthma and has never had the opportunity to develop skills for the paid labor market. Mrs. Hayes now lives on welfare and food stamps because the courts have decided that Mr. Hayes should not pay more than $200 per month in spousal support. His annual income is $40,332 (Weitzman, 1985).

Members of the legal profession also engage in an intense debate over the value of household services in wrongful death suits or personal injury cases where the housewife/mother is so incapacitated that she is not able to perform her duties in the home, including consortium (sexual services, companionship). In theory, this is all gender-neutral, as is the divorce court's "supported spouse" language. That is, a woman should be able to receive compensation for her husband's household services in a wrongful death suit. Significant male participation in housework is still so unlikely that a woman requesting such compensation would probably have to have "proof" of such services. Field (1989) summarizes 33 articles in an issue of *The Professional Reader* devoted to "The Value and Worth of Housewives and Household Activities." Only one article out of 33 directly indicates that men might be involved in housework.

Figure 1, which documents reasons for not being in the labor force for women and men, reveals the enormous disparity between women and men when it comes to housework. This state of affairs leads to the conclusion that housework and childcare are regarded as work when the worker in question is either dead or incapacitated, and the man loses the services of his wife. A strange and convenient (for men) definition of work, indeed.

In fact, prostitution, like marriage, is seen as the economic fall-back position for all women no matter their age, status, or desire. And sometimes it is difficult to distinguish marriage from prostitution since "it is merely a question of degree whether she sells herself to one man, in or out of marriage, or to many men" (Goldman, 1970).

It should, therefore, come as a surprise to no one that prostitutes and housewives have formed alliances in such organizations as Wages for Housework, and the Alliance for the Safety of Prostitutes in Canada, and the United States Prostitutes' Collective (Bell, 1987).

Fig. 1. Reasons for not being in the labor force by sex, 1975 and 1988[1]

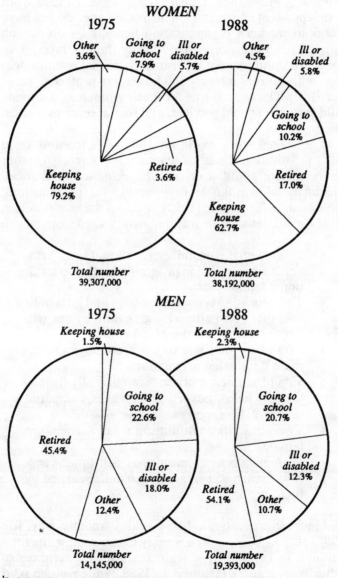

WOMEN

1975

Other 3.6%
Going to school 7.9%
Ill or disabled 5.7%
Keeping house 79.2%
Retired 3.6%
Total number 39,307,000

1988

Other 4.5%
Ill or disabled 5.8%
Going to school 10.2%
Retired 17.0%
Keeping house 62.7%
Total number 38,192,000

MEN

1975

Keeping house 1.5%
Going to school 22.6%
Retired 45.4%
Ill or disabled 18.0%
Other 12.4%
Total number 14,145,000

1988

Keeping house 2.3%
Going to school 20.7%
Ill or disabled 12.3%
Retired 54.1%
Other 10.7%
Total number 19,393,000

[1]Includes only persons out of the labor force by choice.

Source: U.S. Bureau of Labor Statistics, January 1976, Table 29 and January 1989, Table A-54.

However, the marginal status of women in the waged work world does not offer much promise to women organizing around wages and benefit issues for housewives and prostitutes. Prostitutes in the legal brothels in Nevada work as independent contractors. This means they do not have access to workers' compensation benefits for on-the-job injuries, health insurance paid for by the employer, pensions or unemployment insurance (personal communications with sources whose confidences are protected, Summer 1990). The same is true for many women who provide child care, household services, and sexual services (Enloe, 1989).

The waged work world does not offer freedom from either prostitution or marriage for most women. "Whether our reformers admit it or not, the economic and social inferiority of women is responsible for prostitution" (Goldman, 1970). Deane (1990) provides the now familiar, but still grim statistics for women in the waged work world:

♦ 70% of female secondary vocational school students are enrolled in programs leading to traditional female jobs
♦ The educational choices of boys and girls indicate that occupational segregation by sex will continue well into the 21st century
♦ 77% of women workers are employed in female-dominated occupations
♦ 43% of women workers are currently in jobs that pay below poverty level wages, compared to only 27% of men
♦ Two out of three minimum wage earners are female
♦ Women workers, employed full-time, year-round, earn 65 cents for each dollar earned by men (p. 30)

Figure 2 presents the harsh reality another way. Rix (1990) states, "The median weekly earnings of white men continue to exceed, by a wide margin, the earnings of minority men and all women. In 1988, white women who

Fig. 2. Median usual weekly earnings of full-time wage and salary workers by sex, race, and Hispanic origin, 1988 (in dollars)

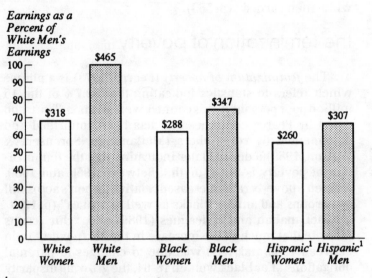

[1]Persons of Hispanic origin may be of any race.

Source: U.S. Bureau of Labor Statistics, January 1989, Table 61.

worked full-time had median weekly earnings of $318, approximately 68% of the $465 median earnings of full-time working white men. Black and Hispanic women fared even worse, earning, respectively, only 62% and 56% of what white men earned" (p. 360).

the feminization of poverty

The *feminization of poverty* (Pearce, 1978) is a phrase which refers to statistics indicating that 62.7% of the 15 million poor persons in this country were women. The trend noted by Pearce continues and has been confirmed and documented by researchers (McLanahan, Sorensen, & Watson, 1989) a decade later indicating that the feminization of poverty is not a myth. "Between 1950 and 1980, women's poverty rates increased relative to men's across all age groups and among Blacks as well as whites" (p. 121).

McLanahan and colleagues (1989) add, "Our results indicate that much of the increase in the sex/poverty ratio between 1960 and 1980 was due to changes in parental obligations...For Black women 18-64, the growing disparity in parental responsibility accounted for about 70% of the increase in the sex/poverty ratio. For white women 25-64, it accounted for about 86% of the increase in the ratio" (p. 127).

The combination of the economic consequences of divorce and the reality of women's marginal position in the waged work world are examples of structural violence against women and their children, who would be completely abandoned if not for the heroic efforts of their mothers to provide for them despite the odds (Long-Scott, 1990).

And finally, Giobbe (1990) states, "By maintaining a society in which women are kept economically marginalized, the system of male supremacy ensures that a pool of women will be vulnerable to recruitment and entrapment in prostitution" (p. 4).

so what do we tell our daughters?

I pushed Enloe's (1989) book, *Bananas, Beaches & Bases: Making Feminist Sense of International Politics*, into the hands of a Iranian friend who is a computer scientist, playwright, and father of an adolescent daughter. I thought he, as a world traveler and intellectual, might find the book interesting. He paged through it thoughtfully, looked up and said, "But she stresses the importance of *secretaries* in global politics! What am I supposed to tell my daughter? Become a secretary?" (F. Nateghian, personal communication, October 24, 1990).

I advised him that he had put his finger on the entire problem of talking about women and work. The problem lies not in the work but in *who* does the work. If women do it, it's devalued. The work, somehow, becomes contaminated by women's participation (Louise, 1980).

This then puts a woman in an impossible situation. If she does not want to become a secretary or a nurse or a teacher or participate in female work ghettos along with the other 77% of working women, is she a betrayer of all those other women? Does she devalue the work of other women in order to become a manager or an attorney? Such choices, of course, are confined to affluent white women and those few women of color who have somehow slipped through to become tokens within the white female professional and managerial ranks (Amott & Matthaei, 1991).

For some women, this betrayal and subsequent isolation has made it impossible for them to leave the clerical track, even when the opportunity is offered and the advantages are apparently clear. As an employer of women, I was stunned by the inability of women to take the career ladder offered to them in my company. Part of the reason for writing this book is to understand why this should be so.

Trying to sing the praises of secretarial work has a bogus quality much like the feeling one gets when African-Americans claim that Thomas Jefferson was black or when lesbians claim Eleanor Roosevelt as one of their own. It's a sense of embarrassment. As though lesbians and African-Americans and secretaries and housewives have no identity of their own and are trying to claim one by latching onto someone or something which has a recognized identity in the patriarchal world.

Or perhaps the embarrassment arises from discovering what Minnich (1990) describes as root errors in patriarchal thinking. The most basic is faulty generalization. This is the business of accepting only male people as the ones who are significant, the only ones who can set the standard for all other people. Minnich writes on the concept of woman as "the human creature who is different from man with regard to reproductive function while men were not defined exclusively with regard to their reproductive role" (p. 122). She continues, "To achieve genuine equality, to approach real comprehension of women, man must be deuniversalized so that our own meanings can emerge, and can do so in plural and in differentiated terms. We cannot be equal until we can be different in our own ways, not those imposed on us" (p. 123).

So what do we tell our daughter(s)? We tell her that we support *her* in whatever her work is. We tell her that she has an *identity* as a worker whether she works in the waged or unwaged realms of productive activity. We demand that she have all the privileges and rewards of a worker. We move our focus from the shifting and slippery definitions of work and we turn our gaze on *her*. We enter her world of work, her experience. We accept her as a *being-in-the-world.*

Sounds so simple, doesn't it? The language is so attractive, so powerful and yet, still so unavailable for women. The phrase *being-in-the-world* is a term in phenomenological psychology and psychiatry defined as two poles–self and the world. The self implies world and world self; there is neither without the other, and each is understandable only in terms of the other (May, 1983).

Honoring another person's experience of self and the world is the very foundation of the women's movement, the true meaning of consciousness raising, a restatement of the feminist dictum: The personal is the political.

So I was drawn to the *being-in-the-world* concept as a way to approach my research, to do the long interviews with women abuse survivors, to satisfy my desire to raise the voices of women about their work.

I rushed to the library where I found May's (1983) book, *The Discovery of Being: Writings in Existential Psychology.* May writes:

> The problem is how we are to understand the other person's world. It cannot be understood as an external collection of objects which we view from the outside (in which case we never really understand it), nor by sentimental identification (in which case our understanding doesn't do any good, for we have failed to preserve the reality of our own existence). A difficult dilemma indeed! What is required is an approach to the world which undercuts the "cancer"—namely, the traditional subject-object dichotomy. (pp. 117-118)

Okay. So far, so good.

May (1983) then goes on to describe how "Western *man* ...has lost his sense of being. The existential analysts believe there is much evidence that...twentieth century Western man not only experiences an alienation from the human world about him but also suffers an inner, harrowing conviction of being estranged (like, say, a paroled convict) in the natural world as well" (p. 118).

For readers who are trying to read *she's* and *her's* into all those *he's, him's,* and *his's,* give it up. May (1983) reveals his true perspective by describing a 1934 case study of "Ruldolf, the butcher boy who shot a prostitute" (p. 124-125). Ruldolf became a patient to the existential analyst, Roland Kuhn, after he shot the prostitute and surrendered himself to the police. May uses this case to describe what he apparently considers as exemplary therapy. Kuhn discovers that Rudolf has never properly mourned the death of his mother, and so Kuhn enters the "world of the mourner" along with his patient.

And then...May (1983) quoting Kuhn quoting Rilke, "Killing is one of the forms of our wandering mourning" (p. 124).

And then we know that women as beings have been dismissed. And then we know that the foot soldiers, the cannon fodder among us in the sex war have been deemed expendable. And all we know about the prostitute is: "She was hit by the bullet but only slightly injured." Neither May nor Kuhn gives *her* a second glance, another word. She is neither sentimentally identified nor placed in a collection of external objects. The subject/object dichotomy is not to be found anywhere when it comes to *her* being-in-the-world, or in the bar where Rudolf found *her*, or in front of a gun where Rudolf shot *her*. We don't even know her name.

What would May have to say about the Montreal massacre? Was Marc Lepine also in a "state of wandering mourning?" Is it important to recognize Lepine's status as a being-in-the-world? Is this why his name is always used in the accounts of this tragedy and not the names of the women he murdered? The collapse of the private world of women and women's work into the public sphere means that women are now beings-in-the-world as never before. Therefore, although *The New York Times* and *The San Francisco Chronicle* erased the names of the slain at the University of Montreal, I do not. These are our daughters, our sisters, and these are their names (Edwards, 1990; Williams, 1989):

Genevieve Bergeron, 21
Helene Colgan, 23
Nathalie Croteau, 23
Barbara Diagneault, 22
Anne-Marie Edward, 21
Maude Haviernick, 29
Barbara Maria Klueznick, 31
Maryse Leclaire, 23
Maryse Langaniere, 25
Anne-Marie Lemay, 22
Sonia Pelletier, 28
Michele Richard, 21
Annie St. Arneault, 23
Annette Turcotte, 21

the purpose of this book

Qualitative research methods (described in detail in Appendix 1) were essential to this study because, as one of the rape survivors put it: *Nobody ever asked me about my work before.* This is the statement of a woman who has always worked in the waged labor market, who has been interviewed by electronic and print media journalists, and who lost an entire profession because of her abuse experience. Her obvious relief at my interest in how the marital rape and battering trauma had affected her worklife led to the revelation that previous scrutiny about her experience by journalists had bordered on the voyeuristic, the pornographic. Her identity as a worker was neither recognized nor explored.

The purpose of this book is to identify women as workers, to explore the impact of abuse on that identity, and to suggest how vocational rehabilitation methods and expertise can be used to assist women in healing their work lives.

*My grandfather would have
me take razor blades and cut
him. He would have me cut
him on his paralyzed side. He
would shoot me up with morphine and molest me.*

–from *Laura's Story*

laura's story*

I'm still so disbelieving that I'm...the silent survivor.
Survivors exist in silence. That's how the abuse happened and so I can't believe what I'm finding out. I
grew up alone in myself. I can't believe I'm actually
part of a group of other people, sharing that same
aloneness growing up.

My life is a life of terror and I'm trying not to feel it.
And sometimes I'm exploring that I could be a
multiple person. I don't know if I fit into the categories,
but I've lost time. One part of me, yeah, believes the
whole fuckin' world is a hustle and a con. That's what
I'm out for. That's what I do as a prostitute. I'm 40 now.
I've been a prostitute for 20 years.

I come from a wealthy family. My mother lives in
Arizona and my father and stepmother live in Boston.
My younger sister lives in Sedona near my mother.
We're white. My parents got divorced when I was five
years old. My mother had a trust so she never worked
except volunteer society stuff and my father was into
finance.

I have a few flashes before the age of seven but
that's it. I remember being seven and coming to in
the living room with a rock-and-roll station on, loud,
and I was masturbating. I had just finished and my
mother walked in and started raging about how she
didn't want me listening to that kind of music. Then it
turned out that I had a best friend. I don't know where
she came from or anything. I don't know what grade
I was in.

One other memory—being in a ballet class when
I was five and a half. They were doing "Swan Lake"
and I was flunking. I was not able to go on to the next
ballet. I had to repeat "Swan Lake" with a new
group of kids coming in. I was totally uncoordinated.
There was a lot of shame.

A memory of being punished—of having to sit
from eight at night to one in the morning because I
wouldn't eat my peas, carrots, spinach, beets. I know

*In her own words.

I was past four. My mother came down every half hour to make sure I was eating my food. There were no lights on. I wasn't even entitled to have lights in the kitchen. There were two dogs on either side of my high chair or raised chair that I sat at. Finally, I knew the only way I was going to get out of there was to go throw up. So I ate them and threw up.

In the fourth grade, I was drawing a picture of flowers in a vase. The teacher came by and said, "It doesn't look like that." I never drew again.

Then sixth grade, dancing with all the girls in the class to records in June before school let out. It was 110 degrees and I came to in the sunlight, dancing. Everything else had been dead and blank, blackness.

Kindergarten. My mother told a therapist we went to that I had been sent to a parochial school and the nun kept calling my mother and saying that I was totally withdrawn. "Something's wrong with her. I can't get her to interact with any of the kids." All I remember is being inside a cubby hole with a blanket. I spent most of my time there.

Two months or so ago somebody said something in my AA group which triggered a memory of the first grade. A boy climbing a jungle gym and me climbing the jungle gym and the boy running up and shouting, "I can see your underpants! I can see your underpants!" I went and hid in the cloakroom. They had to force me to go to recess.

About 10 years ago, I saw that TV movie, "Something About Amelia." I saw myself in school. It wasn't so much the sexual part but the emotional part. How she was emotionally devastated, and in school, that's how I was. I just could not believe I was watching myself on TV. After the movie, they flashed a lot of stuff about where to get help. I thought, "I'll have to go to an incest group although this didn't happen to me, I see myself in this."

For about four or five years, maybe three years—times are confusing to me; I got into Al-Anon because of my boyfriend. He battered me and he shot up heroin. He said he could never get married so long as he was with me. I work as a prostitute. I only see him three times a year and I'm bi-sexual. The whole thing was ridiculous. So I went into my first

12-Step Program and then I find out that there are incest meetings within blocks of the 12-Step meetings. So I started going to incest meetings.

I figured I belonged in those meetings, not because anybody had done anything maliciously to me, but because of my 10 operations between the age of seven months to 18 months of age. When I was doing re-birthing, I was constantly on the operating table. My urine was reflexing back into my kidneys. I was nearly blue before my mother took me in. I was catheterized continually. When I was older I always had these bladder infections. Anyway, they cut my clitoris in one of the operations by accident. When people go down on you or touch you? This is supposed to be a wonderful experience for women? I nearly go through the roof. It feels like somebody scratching on a chalkboard. The first incest meeting I went to—it was terrible. I cried through the whole thing. I looked at everybody. They looked like fucking losers, every woman in that group. They all looked like the women I had spent my entire life in school trying to not be associated with. The losers. The nerds. I was always trying to pretend I wasn't one of them. Now I have to admit that I'm one of you. It was devastating. I stayed for three months and dealt with the operations and the doctor stuff. The doctors were very rough with me. So then I thought I was done.

I ended up at some other meeting after having had a fight with my sister who had lied about me, and I started talking about lying. I had this feeling. I had felt it before. Then the next thing that came out of my mouth, in slow motion, I didn't know it was me. But I heard a voice say: "My grandfather touched me." And then I saw blood in front of my eyes. Blood came flooding down like somebody had slit my eyes, and I saw my grandfather standing up in his wheelchair in my bedroom. Screaming at me that I had disturbed his sleep, that he couldn't sleep. There were bars on the bed.

That night I had dreams of my grandfather attacking me. I was in a terror to get away from him and then I was at the top of the stairs. All of the sudden he was in his chair and I tried to get him to go downstairs and leave me alone. I looked at the chair, and he fell. He fell down this steep flight of stairs and I heard every crack, every time he hit a step. My baby sister was behind me and I told her to go call the hospital because I had killed him, but then he managed to get up, crawl into this car, and drive away.

He was in his eighties when he molested me. I was somewhere between two and a half and four years old. He was in a wheelchair but he could stand up. He was in advanced stages of alcoholism. He was a stroke victim from the alcoholism. He was in dementia. I got all this information from my mother, of course. Anyway, he had around-the-clock nurses because he was so crazy. My mother had moved me into my sister's room and he was in my room. They put bars on my bed so he wouldn't fall out. So my dream was true, except I didn't kill him but when I was being punished, I was told by my mother that I would cause him a stroke if I interfered with his sleep. And he did die after one of my punishments.

My grandfather would have me take razor blades and cut him. He would have me cut him on his paralyzed side. He would shoot me up with morphine and molest me. He had access to morphine for himself. He would sit in his chair and he would have me take the needle and gouge it into his legs. When I would see the blood and stuff, he would laugh hysterically because it would upset me. My grandfather made me pose for him. I'd have to lift up my dress and stick my hand down my pants. I'd have to strike all these seductive poses. He would have me strip for him. He told me I was his little performer, his star. He was going to make me a star. He said he was a director and he would play the camera game which is pretending to have a camera at one's eye and cranking it. He was going to give me all this money. The actual molest, the physical stuff was...I'd be sitting on his knees facing out and he would turn the rock-and-roll station up real loud, and jab his cock into my butt. Not into the anus, but pushing on the cheek. He told me that when I was bigger, he wanted to stick it in. He would come on my butt. He peed on me. He would get my hair wet with urine. He told me I would be killed...everybody I loved would be killed.

When I was four, my mother sent me to my room. My grandfather was gone by then. He had died. I must have said something. She washed my mouth out with soap. She didn't let me out of my room for two weeks. My sister was not allowed to talk to me. My father was out of the house because my parents were separated. My mother wouldn't have anything to do with me. She told me I was a bad girl. I was aced out. I died. I remember screaming for two days, solid. Screaming, crying. Nobody came for me. This blackness just came over me. Then after two weeks, my mother dragged me and my sister to a priest who harangued us for two hours about...well, I knew it was sexual, and that I was being punished for that. My mother came to pick us up and when I came back, I was no longer a bad person. I was totally subservient. I had lost my identity. I had to be for my mother. I was her slave after that, a good girl.

I asked my mother about it when I went to incest group and she screeched at the top of her lungs, "It never happened!" I think it did. My mother says it was my father, "I tried to keep you away from him."

Before I started prostitution, from about 15 on, guys kept coming on to me. I started hitchhiking a lot. I was constantly having to jump out of cars because guys would fondle me, offer to give me money, want me to fondle them. Before I jumped out of the car, I would do what they wanted me to do. I would lift up my blouse. I would stick my hands into my pants. I would strike seductive poses. I would just keep posing. When they tried to take my hand and put it on them, I would go numb, and then I'd get out of the car. Eventually, I'd yell, "What kind of girl do you think I am?" I'd jump out and scream and run away. I had a boyfriend when I was 13. I don't know how I ever managed to have him. I don't know where he came from. He would try to kiss me, and I would pump up my veins and pretend I was shooting up heroin. Then I would nod out. That was the go-ahead for him to try to kiss me and stuff. This never made any sense to me until I remembered about my grandfather.

When I finally got away from home, I would fuck. Twenty guys a day. Hundreds and hundreds of guys. I would take downers to come down. I couldn't smoke pot because it'd make me schizophrenic. I gave gonorrhea to everybody. I had to have surgery later because I screwed up my tubes. I was reliving the abuse but I didn't know it.

I worked as an artist's model but it was real boring. I loved working for a camera. I never felt so high or so good. I couldn't get into porno movies because I looked too much like a hippie. I ventured into loops but I didn't like that either. Loops are 15-minute hardcore stuff for porn booths. I had two straight jobs. I tried a couple of times to be a waitress but I could not function. I mean, I'm really intelligent, but I couldn't keep the orders straight. I got fired or quit many jobs after a day or two. I was unable to function. It never made any sense to me. Why couldn't I keep anything straight? When I was 12 or 13, I had a nervous breakdown. I was flipping out and I was unable to concentrate on the page, on any written words. In school, I wore peter pan collars, no makeup. I looked like I was in the second grade. I spent the entire 7th grade in the girls' bathroom. I would sit with my face to the wall, and then the girls would come in and out. I would pretend to comb my hair. Pretend I was invisible, act as though I belonged there. I would pray for them to leave. When I got home at night, I would lock myself into my room and play a Rolling Stones' song, "Mona," over and over. I played it as loud as I could, and I would scream. I screamed for hours.

I've been in experimental high schools, colleges, mental hospitals. A friend of mine found me in San Francisco. I was sick with VD, malnutrition. He put me on the plane to the East Coast, to my father's house. I left there and I went to New York City. I lived in a shooting gallery. I would tie them off, they'd shoot up, go into the bathroom, throw up, and I'd tie them again. I lived off other people's highs. I was going to secretarial school. I quit and got a job filing for $65.00 per week. I had multiple bosses. There was this disgusting hierarchy with the secretaries. The flowers and kissing up to the bosses. They'd go to the Playboy Club at night and I'd hear about it the next day. Talking about squeezing the tits, getting a cock-feel off the bunnies. Idiots.

I had seen these ads for massage parlors. I went in for an interview. It was just like a regular office. The guy

said I could set my own hours around my file clerk job.
The first blow job I ever gave was on a high table. I
ended up with my head hanging over. The guy was
real tall. He rammed his cock down my throat from
above. It was like I was a rag doll. He came that way.
I threw up, gagged, and coughed. Then I came to.
I was never in that position again. I wanted the
control. I wanted on top. My body changed. I took
part in it. I quit my file clerk job. I could get $18.00 per
hour just for a straight massage? I'm WORTH THAT
MUCH? Now the bosses who treated me like scum in
the office, came in as tricks, immature nobodies.
They all become little boys. They give you power. It's
phenomenal. I took it.

You know, I've never been able to say the word
"whore" or "whorehouse" until I got a memory
back about my grandfather talking about
whorehouses. Now I can say I work in a whorehouse.
Being able to say this just happened three months
ago.

I plan to keep working. Some prostitutes I know
are 50, even 60. I think people in the sex industry stay
younger, longer. I'm writing a film script about prostitution in Nevada. I want to show the day-to-day
living, the girl in her room with the tricks. These guys
are regular guys, you know, your husbands and
boyfriends. I want to produce it or be part of the
production. I'm not afraid of any of those Hollywood
types. I've dealt with them. They're just as idiotic as
anybody. I have books I want to write. I'd like my own
movie company but I'm a ways from that.

I like working in Nevada, but the hours are getting
to me now, the 14-hour shifts. When I leave the
brothel, I have all these flashbacks and suicidal
memories of my grandfather telling me to kill myself.
In the brothel I've created a structured environment
for myself, I cannot fall apart there.

one

prostitution as the center of the rape paradigm

So I tried to make a category. I really did try. But by then I was beginning to have an impossible time with classification (Morgan, 1989, p. 331).

As if women's lives could be chopped up into these little bits. Some economic punishment over here, and over there... all these different perpetrator names, too: a little bio-dad incest, a little stepfather incest, boy-down-the-street child abuse, day care provider/nap-time abuse. We've got lists and proliferations of occasions ... all over the map. Sometimes it's real hard to keep all this straight. I find myself that I keep getting these categories mixed up. Sexual harassment starts looking like battery, starts looking like incest. Here's the camera. It starts looking like pornography. Oh no! It looks like the First Amendment. I'm told that I'm a pretty good lawyer. One of the habits of mind that's supposed to make you into a good lawyer, is that these categories are supposed to make a kind of gut-level sense. You look at this array of words and you go, "Oh, home! I'm here. I understand." Also, you're

*supposed to know that other things can't be catego-
rized. They won't fall into categories, so you won't try
that. So, rape is rape. Say it ten times: Incest is incest
and prostitution is prostitution, and nobody can know
what pornography is! The categories are supposed to
match up with something that's real in the world...This
not being able to keep my categories straight presented me with something of a professional crisis. Then
I go into my classroom, feminist theory class, and one
of my students starts calling incesting fathers "johns"
which tells me that it's not only my problem. And as I
start looking at the women whose lives I'm representing in court, and looking at all of them all at one time,
and it's looking to me more like one long gang bang,
and a whole lot less than one from Column A and one
from Column B (Baldwin, 1990).*

And I thought it was just me. When I started putting this book together, I thought I would divide it into rape, battering, and incest. It had a nice internal logic starting from abuse which happened in the world (e.g., stranger rape in the bushes) to battering inside the home, to the heart and secret of the family, incest. I ran into problems immediately. What should I do with marital rape? Does it go under wife battering or rape? What about teacher child abuse? Is it rape or some form of incest? Where would I put child battering with and without incest? What about date rape, also known as acquaintance rape? What about ritual abuse? Abuse by mothers? Siblings? Abuse of the disabled? Lesbian battering? Sexual harassment?

When I started interviewing my co-researchers, I found experiences which had no category at all. For example, what shall we call Harriet's experience of finding an identified rapist, but not *her* rapist, shot dead on the patio of her apartment? Sexual terrorism?

My co-researchers' lives, as well as my own life, are testimony to the multiple abuse experiences women appear to have throughout their lives. It no longer seems possible to simply identify oneself as a rape survivor or incest victim. When I attended the national conference of the National Coalition Against Domestic Violence (NCADV) in Amherst, Massachusetts in August 1990, I found I was excluded from the Formerly Battered Women's Institute because I was not a formerly battered woman. As a well-trained feminist, I know it is politically correct to allow oppressed groups to organize around their own oppression, so I meekly accepted my exclusion. Then I started thinking: wait a minute, as an incest survivor, am I not a victim of family violence? What if I had had to watch my mother being beaten while I was growing up? Would I be excluded, too? I complained to a woman standing in front of me in the cafeteria line. She told me she was an incest survivor, too, but that she had gone to the Formerly Battered Women's Institute anyway. Then I felt stupid because I had not used my hard-won assertiveness skills learned back in the 1970s.

"It no longer seems possible to simply identify oneself as a rape survivor or incest victim."

Before the Amherst conference, I had attended the national conference of the National Coalition Against Sexual Assault (NCASA) in July 1990 in Denver, Colorado. Incest survivors were accepted under the umbrella of sexual assault as a category. I felt right at home because my acquaintance rape experience fit in there, too. But although there was a workshop on rape as part of the battering experience at the NCADV conference, marital rape did not appear as a category or workshop or formal topic anywhere within the five-day NCASA conference in Denver. (Diana E. H. Russell's [1990] seminar, "From Witches to Bitches: Sexual Terrorism Against Women," did include information on marital rape as part of the seminar material, but not as a separate category.)

Sexual harassment appears to have been taken over by NCASA as their issue but NCADV does not address it. What if you work for your husband in his (yours and his) business and he rapes you on the job? What conference would you attend? Would you start a new category? A new organization?

What have I missed? Oh, emotional abuse and battery fit in here somewhere, but like Morgan (1989), I'm having an impossible time with classification.

How did we get into this muddle? What do we do about it? Why do we have to do anything about it at all?

There are at least three reasons for this chaos. One is that when we started out, we had little understanding that women's abuse histories are stories of continued and multiple abuse experiences. Our response to abuse was based on an understanding of abuse experiences as isolated and separate events in a woman's life. Even when we understood that a woman had a history of incest as well as rape, for example, we had not yet connected the significance of this in any wholistic way.

Child battering was brought to the foreground in the 1960s by social workers. The feminist response to abuse issues started with the anti-rape movement surfacing in the 1970s, followed quickly by the battered women's movement (Schechter, 1982). In the 1980s, the focus was on stabilizing funding for shelters and rape crisis services, and in developing techniques to deal with the resulting legal tangle we had wrought. This is best exemplified in both the expansion of rape categories (e.g., the inclusion of marital rape), and in the legal testing of new psychological injury categories–Battered Woman Syndrome (BWS) and Rape Trauma Syndrome (RTS)–emerging under Post-traumatic Stress Disorder (PTSD) which was inserted into the Diagnostic and Statistical Manual of Mental Disorders (DSM) in 1980.

The 1980s also saw an information explosion in abuse studies with the proliferation of research on abuse issues as well as the publication of reputable books and articles documenting the characteristics of abuse experiences. Lenore Walker's classic book, *The Battered Woman*, was published in 1979, and followed by the testing of her theories in the Battered Woman Syndrome model (Campbell, 1990). Diana E. H. Russell (1982, 1984, 1986) published the results of her San Francisco study in at least three books on incest, marital rape, sexual harassment, and rape. Even male academics, such as Finkelhor and associates (Finkelhor, Gelles, Hotaling, & Straus, 1983; Finkelhor & Yllo, 1985) and Straus (1988) began to publish on these topics. Survivor literature became so pervasive that Louise Armstrong (1978), the author of *Kiss Daddy Goodnight: A Speak-out on Incest*, complained about the political value of such documents in the March 1990 issue of *The Women's Review of Books*.

Therefore, the second reason we are all having this trouble with categories appears to be an information glut. This is not to say we have the truth or that everything has been understood and documented, but that we are having a difficult time even managing what we know so far. The problem of abuse appears to be deeper, wider, more violent, and more pervasive than we ever guessed in the beginning days of the women's movement. It is my position that we are still not home, to bedrock. Hopefully, the 1990s will see us get there.

The third reason for our muddle is a familiar one. It is the business of trying to apply the patriarchal paradigm to women's lives. Since this is the dominant paradigm as expressed in all the disciplines, including religion, law, education, media, and most of all, science, it is hardly surprising that we continue to try to fit our approach to abuse dynamics within this paradigm.

The dominant paradigms in scientific thought are challenged by such critics as Kuhn (1970). Kuhn's *The Structure of Scientific Revolutions* grapples with definitions of "paradigm" and paradigm shift. A paradigm is a model or a pattern. A paradigm shift is not to be confused with change. For example, a change in dictators or in marriage by trading one batterer for another is just a change, not a fundamental transformation or paradigm shift. The pattern remains.

Feminism is, of course, an alternative paradigm to the dominant paradigm of patriarchy which now rests on the scientific method. The table of contents of Kuhn's (1970) book can be read as an outline of the paradigm shift process for both scientific and feminist revolutions. A simple substitution of the word "patriarchy" for the word "science" works quite well.

Some of the characteristics of paradigm shift include "a challenge to the dominant paradigm by thinkers who have created an unprecedented achievement (the women's movement) attracting enduring groups of adherents (feminists) away from competing modes of scientific activity (patriarchy). Simultaneously, it (feminist thought) was sufficiently open-ended to leave all sorts of problems for the redefined group of practitioners (feminists) to resolve" (Kuhn, 1970, p. 10). Other characteristics of a paradigm shift include confronting the invisibility of the dominant paradigm (patriarchy), and the resistance to alternative paradigms (feminism) by the adherents of the dominant paradigm (patriarchy). The rape paradigm and the feminist challenge to it demonstrate the paradigm shift process.

The problem of abuse appears to be deeper, wider, more violent, and more pervasive than we ever guessed in the beginning days of the women's movement.

The rape paradigm is as follows:

1. Very small groups of women are classified as rapable–virginal white women who are perceived as the property of white males (Baldwin, 1990).
2. Large groups of women are classified as unrapable. That is, everybody else: married women, women and girls who have been raped before, all women of color, women who have had sex, prostitutes and women perceived as prostitutes (Baldwin, 1990).

3. In the United States, all African-American men want to rape all white women. By implication this extends to all men of color (Brownmiller, 1975).
4. Women choose, want, enjoy, like being raped (Dworkin, 1989).
5. Women lie about being raped (Largen, 1988).
6. Women are not injured by rape (Ledray, 1988).

The feminist challenge to the rape paradigm to date is:

1. Expansion of the classification of rapable women. Addition of acquaintance, date, family rape (incest), and marital rape to the stranger rape category (Brownmiller, 1975; Dworkin, 1976, 1989; Dworkin & MacKinnon, 1988; Finkelhor & Yllo, 1985; Russell, 1982, 1984, 1986).
2. Contraction of the classification of unrapable women. Prostitutes are not included in this contraction. Rape shield laws do not protect them (Baldwin, 1990). (Rape shield laws prevent a woman's past sexual history from being introduced in a criminal proceeding as part of the defense strategy for an alleged rapist.)
3. Identification of the actual historical rape of enslaved African-American women by white men. By implication this includes all women of color (Brownmiller, 1975).
4. A partial rejection of the "choice" model of rape. Unless prostitution and pornography are included within the feminist challenge to the rape paradigm, rape will be seen as a choice (Hunter & Reed, 1990).
5. The evolution of rape shield laws in the courts in an effort to bolster women's credibility. Or the attempt to overcome Freud's dictum that abuse survivors were having fantasies (Largen, 1988).
6. Women are injured by rape. Emergence of the Post-traumatic Stress Disorder Category in the

DSM-III (American Psychiatric Association, 1987). Emergence of domestic tort law and civil suits brought by rape survivors (Karp & Karp, 1989; Kilpatrick, Veronen & Best, 1985).

As Kuhn (1970) would put it, feminists have "all sorts of problems" which remain to be solved. Not the least of these is the untenable moral position described by Baldwin (1990) as "the trickle-down theory of feminism." Baldwin is referring to the feminist paralysis on the issues of prostitution and pornography. (For purposes of this discussion, I do not distinguish between pornography and prostitution. I agree with Dworkin and MacKinnon [1988] in seeing pornography as something which is done to women used in systems of prostitution.)

To construct prostitution as a choice of employment for women is to ignore the childhood rape of this class of women which ranges from 65% to 85% depending on the study (Neland, undated; Silbert & Pines, 1982). Clinicians place the figure nearer to 100% (private conversations with Reno, Nevada psychologists, January 1991). The child rape of females is considered a prerequisite to preparation for a life of prostitution by pimps who assert, "We are not to blame, we only pick up the girls where their fathers have left off" (Barry, 1991, p. 4).

Women used in systems of prostitution may not be able to connect their childhood abuse to their prostitution experience. This means that prostitutes themselves may be convinced of prostitution as a choice. Such realities are well documented in *Laura's Story*. One of the ways to survive child rape and torture is to "forget" that it ever happened. Laura has been in prostitution for 20 years and she recalled her child rape only three years ago. She is still not in possession of all of her memories. In other words, women used in prostitution are no different from other childhood rape and incest survivors in suppressing their trauma (Silbert & Pines, 1982). The separation of prostitution from child rape and torture is to support the rape paradigm (see numbers 2, 4, 5, 6 above.) The construction and general acceptance of prostitution as work in the legal brothels of Nevada means that the patriarchy has succeeded in legitimizing child abuse.

The rape shield laws were another response to the rape paradigm, particularly number 2, and was designed to protect victims/witnesses from courtroom abuse and to preserve the integrity of the trial system by dictating the relevancy of evidence to the courts (Largen, 1988). There is general agreement that the rape shield provisions which have been adopted in every state have been effective (Largen, 1988). However, the rape shield provisions do not address the reality of women's experiences, which is that of multiple abuse. Therefore, the attorney attempting to assist the court and a jury in understanding why a woman appears to passively acquiesce in her own rape is in an impossible position because the prior abuse history cannot be brought forward. It has now been constructed as irrelevant (Baldwin, 1990).

"We are not to blame, we only pick up the girls where their fathers have left off."

For all practical purposes, prostitutes have been excluded from the rape shield provisions. This fits neatly into the rape paradigm notion that women and girls who have had sex before the rape and who have been raped prior to this particular rape are unrapable. Furthermore, research indicates that prostitutes who try to save themselves from rape injuries by telling their rapists that they are prostitutes experience more injury than those women who were not perceived as prostitutes (Silbert, 1988).

The data surfacing from the Council For Prostitution Alternatives (CPA) in Portland, Oregon and from Women Hurt In Systems of Prostitution Engaged In Revolt (WHISPER) in Minneapolis, Minnesota indicate that the average age of entry into prostitution in the United States is somewhere between 13 and 16 years of age (Neland, undated;

WHISPER, 1990). This brings us back to the rape paradigm and to speculation on why statutory rape law is not applied to this class of very young women. Statutory rape is defined as having sex with minors regardless of "consent." The age of consent varies from state to state.

The CPA (Neland, undated) and WHISPER (1990) also indicate that many young women are extorted into prostitution by the use of pornographic pictures taken by pimps for this purpose. And some women have been BORN into prostitution because they are the daughters of prostitutes who have no control over their own lives let alone the lives of their children (Hunter & Reed, 1990). This combination of child rape, extortion, and being born into prostitution undermines the construction of prostitution as work while supporting the construction of prostitution as slavery.

The other justification for prostitution is that the women make lots, pots, and even bank vaults of money, but the WHISPER (1990) and CPA (Neland, undated) data indicate that the women rarely keep the money they earn. A great deal of money passes through their hands into the hands of pimps and/or "legitimate businessmen" such as the owners of hotels, cab companies, casinos, and legal brothels in Nevada (Baldwin, 1990; Hunter & Reed, 1990; Neland, undated; WHISPER, 1990).

The economic inequality of women can force them into prostitution for survival for themselves and their children (Neland, undated, WHISPER, 1990). Attempts to keep the money by the women can result in battering and death by pimps (who may also be husbands). Demands to be paid for sex can also result in battering and death by customers/ johns (Neland, undated; WHISPER, 1990).

As Susan Kay Hunter (Hunter & Reed, 1990), executive director of the CPA, would ask, "This is choice? Prostitution is a choice?" I would ask, "Is *Laura's Story* a story of choosing prostitution?"

For feminists, putting prostitution at the center of the rape paradigm is a moral imperative, but it also provides tremendous conceptual advantages in approaching all abuse dynamics. By examining the reality of prostitution as violence against women, we have it all. We are at bedrock. As we shall see, every conceivable category of abuse can be discovered in the prostitution experience (S. K. Hunter, personal communication, December 30, 1990; Neland, undated; WHISPER, 1990).

The emergence of prostitution survivors into such groups as CPA and WHISPER provide us with the fulcrum, or as my *Webster's Third Unabridged Dictionary* defines *fulcrum*, "the one who supplies leverage for action." We need to listen to and learn from prostitution survivors.

For feminist rehabilitationists, putting prostitution at the center of the rape paradigm is essential in trying to grasp the nature and extent of abuse injuries. For example, the Gulf War precipitated a state of readiness for the handling of injuries which result from war. A *60 Minutes* (CBS News, 1991) segment reported that stress injuries exceed physical injuries by 10 times for combat soldiers. The report went on to explain procedures for handling stress injuries as close to the front as possible.

Prostitutes are the front-line combat soldiers in the Sex War. Their numbers exceed that of the combat soldiers on the front-lines in the Gulf War, which was estimated at around 500,000 in January 1991 ("How Many Wars," 1991). WHISPER (1990) estimates the number of women actively engaged in prostitution in the United States, at any give time, to be between 500,000 and one million.

Are injuries to prostitutes equivalent to those of combat soldiers? Do prostitutes experience 10 times as many stress injuries as physical injuries? Do battered women, rape survivors, childhood battery and incest survivors experience 10 times as many stress injuries as physical injuries? We don't know. We haven't asked the questions in quite this way before. Isn't it time? In 1980, the number of rape survivors in this country (3,750,000) exceeded the number of combat veterans (2,440,544) (Kilpatrick et al., 1985). It is unlikely that these data include the rape of prostitutes.

Where is the veteran's administration for abuse survivors? What is the state of our readiness? Where are the medics, the doctors, the psychologists, the rehabilitationists?

Money was dangerous to Rhonda. It meant beating, mugging, punishment. Her family, her pimp. They always took the money.

–from *Rhonda's Story*

rhonda's story*

We were an uneasy partnership. She: the woman of color, the injured worker, the former prostitute. Me: the white lady, the vocational rehabilitation counselor, the educated professional. As I huddled with her on the people-eating sofa in front of a television set in the lobby of her psychotherapist's office for more than two hours, I understood that because we were women we were being put in our place. We watched soap operas along with the other women and their children who were also waiting for white male professionals to speak with them. Together, we waited with the muted restlessness of herd animals in a corral.

Rhonda didn't trust me. She trusted her psychotherapist who had been treating her for five years. We were meeting with him so that he could tell her to work with me. She looked to him for reassurance. I was being checked out. Rhonda knew I knew about her having been a prostitute because it was in her file along with psychiatric reports, Minnesota Multiphasic Personality Inventory results, Rorschach tests, re-evaluation of psychiatric status reports, chiropractic reports, and psychotherapy reports.

Rhonda knew I knew about the labels: major depressive episodes, recurrent; psychophysiological disorders including gastritis, stomach pain, and diarrhea; seizure disorders; borderline personality disorder organization; adjustment disorder; malingering; dysthymic disorder; mixed personality disorder; alcohol and heroin abuse dependencies, episodic; sociopathic; hysterical and passive/aggressive; general and chronic physical deterioration; short life expectancy.

Rhonda knew my job was to disengage her from the workers' compensation system; to separate her from her psychotherapist, her chiropractor; to end the five-year flow of workers' compensation disability income; to return her to the straight world where she had

---

* As told by the author.

been blackmailed because of her past as a prostitute. This blackmail led to her breakdown—her stress claim—and tossed her into the workers' compensation system.

Rhonda didn't trust me, but I passed muster with her psychotherapist, and so we went off together to figure it out. Now what?

We had fights. "Cracking gum in machine gun bursts is not going to win over employers, Rhonda." Besides, it was driving me crazy. "Uh, that dress is not appropriate when making job applications." She was still beautiful, sensual with creamy, dark skin and lush breasts. One of those women of color whose ethnicity is not immediately tagged. Caucasian and Mexican-American? Caucasian and African-American? The dress slithered over her body. She got angry on the day of the Big Dress Fight. "What?" Her back was straight. She was all haughty and enraged. I was riveted. I had not seen this aspect of her before. I had been looking. My job was to probe her creatively, to stress her in absentia as the stand-in for potential employers. Where was her strength, her backbone, her self-defense, her uppity? Before the day of the Big Dress Fight, she cried. She sat in my office with me and cried. She sat in her psychotherapist's office with me and cried. She went to the testing center and cried. She cried on the telephone. She cried on the bus. She cried in the street. She cried at the day activity center. She cried over her typewriter.

"What do you want, Rhonda?"

"A room of my own!" she shouted.

I went back to the file to search the records for the facts of her life. I ignored the labels. There was no way for me to process them anyway. I knew there was a deeper truth under the labels, and I found it in the reports and in her endless sorrow. Twenty years of homelessness, hotel rooms, the floors of churches, the street. A lifetime of abuse, childhood battering, adult battering by family members—both male and female, the prostitution history with its life of violence and rape. The tears were ancient. Perhaps childhood rape and torture?

I didn't ask her. Her grief was debilitating. We had NOW to deal with. She didn't live in now. She was drowning in the sorrow of her past, the terror of her future. She wanted a room of her own. I couldn't get *it for her. I got her half. Half of a room with a bed, a nightstand, a wardrobe, a window overlooking an alley, medications handed out daily, meals three times each day, a manager for her money.*

It took me six months to figure it out, and she had to be mugged outside the check cashing storefront for her workers' compensation check before I caught on. Rhonda's connection between work and money had been severed. Money was dangerous to Rhonda. It meant beating, mugging, punishment. Her family, her pimp. They always took the money.

Rhonda could work as long as the work activity was not connected to the making of money. "Rhonda, if anybody asks you, 'what do you do?' Tell them you are a Volunteer with a capital V."

Her workers' compensation settlement is managed by the court who pays the board and care expense directly. Rhonda gets a daily allowance for cigarettes and incidentals. She works as a clerical volunteer at the day activity center. I got a Christmas card from her last year. She says she's happy. I say, she's still alive.

two

the hodgepodge profession: a short history

...there is an assortment of income maintenance, vocational rehabilitation, health care, and social service programs that could, in toto, adequately cover the needs of disabled people. However, their independent histories, separate administrations, turf prerogatives, and inevitable competition for the Federal purse all have effected a fragmented approach to the problems presented by disability. In fact, it can be said that we have no national disability policy per se. Ryan suggests that what is called disability policy is in reality "a variety of policies with different origins and purposes" or "something like a hodgepodge."
(Coudroglou & Poole, 1984, pp. 30-31)

Among the complex network of government programs that offer income support in the United States is a set that provides benefits to disabled persons. In general, disabled women receive less from these public income support programs than do disabled men, despite their often greater economic need. Part

> *of this difference can be attributed to the poor fit*
> *between women's work patterns and the structure of*
> *these programs, and part of the problem lies in the*
> *assumptions about men's and women's economic*
> *and family roles that form the foundation of U.S. public*
> *income transfer programs. Finally, differences between*
> *the ways impaired women and men view themselves*
> *and are viewed by society may account for some of*
> *the gender differences in the receipt of transfer pro-*
> *gram benefits.* (Mudrick, 1988, p. 245)

Rehabilitationists tend to talk to themselves, and I never understood this until a California workers' compensation judge tipped me off about Kafka (H. Lasky, personal communication, July 13, 1982). Kafka's other life was that of an administrator for, and by the time of his retirement, Senior Secretary of the Workmen's Accident Insurance Institute for the Kingdom of Bohemia in Prague. I understand exactly what Kakfa's biographer describes as the "pullulating Austro-Hungarian bureaucracy that like a giant net of near-epic intricacy covered the entire Hapsburg domain" (Pawel, 1984, p. 183).

Historian John Lukas (1990) notes that "traditional capitalism is gone from the West too, even from the United States. The universal attribute of every country in the world is the welfare state, administered by large bureaucracies...the rise of modern bureaucracy is a worldwide phenomenon, something quite different from the Roman or czarist or Prussian bureaucracies of the past" (p. 41).

The vocational rehabilitation profession is part of the modern bureaucratic state and the "near-epic intricacy" of Kafka's world is still with us. The rehabilitation professional now struggles in a network of private sector and public sector programs which require the utmost skill in cautious navigation. Not losing sight of the client in the struggle to manipulate bureaucracy is perhaps the rehabilitationist's greatest challenge, and Kafka's stories are documents of such failures.

This hodgepodge profession emerged from the creation of benefits and services provided to injured and disabled combat soldiers and from the creation of workers' compensation benefits for industrially injured workers (Weed & Field, 1986). In other words, for men.

Given the masculinist origins of the profession, the "poor fit between women's work patterns and the structure ✓ of these programs" is understandable. The following abbreviated history of the profession will reveal the necessity for feminist theory in developing appropriate compensation policies and models for women.

The vocational rehabilitation profession is part of the modern bureaucratic state and the ''near-epic intricacy'' of Kafka's world is still with us.

In the United States, the first rehabilitation program was created by the War Risk Insurance Act of 1914 which provided for the rehabilitation and training of World War I injured veterans. The Smith-Hughes Act of 1917 provided funds for vocational education and was later amended to assist veterans as well (Weed & Field, 1986). Vocational rehabilitation for industrially injured workers was implemented in 1920 with the Smith-Fess Act, which provided for counseling, training, prosthetic appliances, and job placement (Weed & Field, 1986). By 1935, the Social Security Act included a vocational rehabilitation provision (Weed & Field, 1986). This created an ongoing confusion as to what is vocational rehabilitation and what is social welfare. Policy integration among vocational education, job training, and employment programs within social welfare and vocational rehabilitation programs is now minimal to nonexistent (Coudroglou & Poole, 1984). The profession was expanded once again by war with the 1944 Servicemens' Readjustment Act which provided for training, tuition, subsistence, direct loans, unemployment allowances, readjustment benefits, preferential employment, and referral services (Weed & Field, 1986). In succeeding years, funding for graduate training, research, and construction of rehabilitation facilities was increased. Eligibility requirements for rehabilitation services were expanded to include the socially disadvantaged, migrant workers, mentally ill, mentally retarded, the blind, and the severely disabled (Weed & Field, 1986).

The 1970s saw the rise of a civil rights movement by and for the disabled, and the Vocational Rehabilitation Act of 1973 acknowledged the disabled population as consumers of vocational rehabilitation services (Weed & Field, 1986). The Americans With Disabilities Act of 1990 prohibits discrimination based on disability in the areas of employment, public accommodations, government services, transportation and telecommunications. Every employer with more than 25 employees is affected (Americans with Disabilities Act of 1990, P. L. 101-336).

And if the attempt to master separate programs for veterans, civil servants, work-injured people, employed people, and their dependents, and those people who can prove they are sufficiently poor to qualify for benefits is not complex enough, trying to figure out who gets the money and the benefits is even worse. There is neither an agreed-upon definition of disability expenditures nor agreement on how to calculate such expenditures. The total for 1986, in both private and public sectors, was valued at $169.4 billion (Berkowitz & Greene, 1989). Therefore, trying to determine how much of this 169.4 billion dollar pie is going to women is somewhat akin to being the messenger in Kafka's novel, *The Castle*. Like the messenger who starts out everyday to deliver his message, and like Kafka who never finished the book, I never arrive. And I am never finished with Table 1, "Vocational Rehabilitation Delivery Systems by Gender." The data are reflective of the hodgepodge character of the profession. I invite readers to tinker with this table, adding and subtracting as you please. The reason for creating such a table is to give a more graphic representation of how vocational rehabilitation services (e.g., vocational education, medical services, counseling support, and special access to the waged labor market) have been available to men as contrasted to what have been provided to women.

Table 1

Vocational Rehabilitation Delivery Systems on a Gender Continuum*

DATE	FEMALE · · · · · · · · · · · · · · MALE
1914	**War-Risk Act–** Rehabilitation and vocational training.[1]
1917	**Smith-Hughes Act–** Vocational education.[1]
1918	**Soldier Rehabilitation Act–** Vocational education and rehabilitation for disabled veterans.[1]
1920	**Smith-Fess Act–** Counseling, training, job placement, prosthetics to industrially injured.[1]
1935	**Social Security Act–** Vocational Rehabilitation Programs. (In 1970, benefits were still 33% lower for women than men.)[3]
1943	**Borden-LaFollette–** Eligibility expanded for mentally ill and retarded and blind.[1]
1944	**Servicemen's Readjustment Act–** "G.I. Bill"–Training, tuition, subsistence, loans, unemployment allowance, preferential employment.[1,2]
1954	**Vocational Rehabilitation Act–** Emphasis on severely disabled, graduate training, rehabilitation facilities.[1]

(continued on next page)

*All footnotes at end of table.

(Table 1 continued)

DATE	FEMALE · · · · · · · · · · · · · · · MALE	
1965		Vocational Rehabilitation Act– Evaluations extended, services expanded, construction of facilities.[1]
1967	Work Incentive Program WIN– Employment and training for AFDC recipients. Voluntary.[5]	
1968		Vocational Rehabilitation Act– Evaluation and work adjustment for disadvantaged, services to families, follow-up to employment.[1]
1971	WIN becomes mandatory.[4]	
1973		Vocational Rehabilitation Act– Services to severely disabled. Disabled civil rights movement.[1]
	Comprehensive Employment and Training Act (CETA) (Enrollments of women reach 48.5% and 40% under Titles I and II.)[6]	
1974	Supported Work– Structured work experience. AFDC recipients, school dropouts, addicts, ex-offenders.[5]	California Labor Code 139.5– Vocational rehabilitation manda-tory for workers' compensation recipients. (In 1989, women were still only 28.8% of recipients of workers' compensation benefits.)[7]
1975	Displaced Home-maker– California passes the first legisla-tion for work programs.[8]	
1978		Rehabilitation Comprehensive Services and Developmental Disabilities– National research centers funded, independent living services.[1]

(Continued on next page)

(Table 1 continued)

DATE	FEMALE · · · · · · · · · · · · · · · · MALE	
1981	**Omnibus Budget Reconciliation Act (OBRA)– Community Work Experience Program (CWEP)** Workfare–WIN recipients are required to work for AFDC benefits.[5]	
1982	**California Civil Code 4801–** Vocational evaluations for supported spouses in dissolution of marriage cases.[9]	
		Job Training & Partnership Act (JPTA)– Dismantling of CETA. (Racism in form of "creaming" is rampant. Women's needs ignored. 1988.)[6]
1984	**Carl D. Perkins Act–** Vocational education with sex equity, single parent, and home-maker set-asides. (Renewed in 1990.)[10]	
1988	**Family Services Act (FSA) (JOBS)–** Overhaul of AFDC system tying work to welfare.[6]	
1990		**Americans With Disabilities Act (ADA)–** Emphasis on equal access to the workplace.[11]
	Pro Bono Private Sector Vocational Rehabilitation Services to the Battered Women's Movement– Launched at National Coalition Against Domestic Violence National Conference in Amherst, Mass.[12]	

(continued on next page)

Footnotes for Table 1

1. Weed, R. O., & Field, T. (1986, Summer). Differences & similarities between public & private sector vocational rehabilitation: A literature review. *Journal of Applied Rehabilitation Counseling, 17,* 2, 11-14.
2. Berube, A. (1990). *Coming out under fire: The history of gay men and women in world war two* (pp. 228-230). New York: The Free Press. The GI Bill was denied to male veterans with blue or gay discharge papers.
3. Mudrick, N. R. (1988). Disabled women and public policies for income support. In M. Fino & A. Asch (Eds.), *Women with disabilities: Essays in psychology, culture and politics* (p. 257). Philadelphia: Temple University Press.
4. Harlan, S. L. (1989). Welfare, workfare, and training. In S. L. Harlan & R. J. Steinberg (Eds.), *Job training for women: The promise and limits of public policies* (p. 367). Philadelphia: Temple University Press.
5. Gueron, J. M. (1989). Work programs for welfare recipients. In S. L. Harlan & R. J. Steinberg (Eds.), *Job training for women: The promise and limits of public policies* (pp. 365-388). Philadelphia: Temple University Press.
6. Harlan, S. L. (1989). Women and federal job training policy. In S. L. Harlan & R. J. Steinberg (Eds.), *Job training for women: The promise and limits of public policies* (pp. 55-90). Philadelphia: Temple University Press.
7. *California Workers' Compensation Institute Bulletin.* (1990, November 15). No. 90-20. 120 Montgomery St., San Francisco, CA 94104.
8. Miller, J. (1989). Displaced homemakers in the employment and training system. In S. L. Harlan & R. J. Steinberg (Eds.), *Job training for women: The promise and limits of public policies* (pp. 143-165). Philadelphia: Temple University Press.
9. *California Civil Code 4801.* AB2135. C. 514
10. Capitol Update. (1991, Winter). *National business woman,* p. 5.
11. Thompson Publishing Group. (1990). *ADA compliance guide.* Salisbury, MD: Author.
12. Murphy, P. A. (1990, September 5). *Vocational Rehabilitation & Abuse Newsletter.* The Union Institute Center for Women, 1731 Connecticut Ave., #300, Washington, D.C.

In fact, the first work program (the 1967 WIN Program) designed with women in mind was not identified as vocational rehabilitation, was not located within the vocational rehabilitation model, and was basically a response to women's use of AFDC benefits for themselves and their children. Some women took jobs while receiving welfare benefits in order to raise the standard of living for themselves and their children (Harlan, 1989). Instead of allowing welfare mothers (women presumably without men/keepers of their own) to supplement their AFDC incomes by working, the welfare bureaucracy moved in to manage these women's waged and unwaged work lives in much the same way a battering husband or a pimp manages a wife or a prostitute. The needs of children fell by the wayside, and for the first time, mothers were encouraged to work in the waged labor market (Harlan, 1989). The WIN Program can be seen as yet another example of the patriarchy's need to control the definitions of women's work and to gain power over how women structure their waged and unwaged work lives. Services for men, in comparison, were implemented in 1914 as the result of war, and in 1920 as the result of work injuries. This trend flows on and on through World War II and the famous G.I. Bill, to current workers' compensation participation by males at the rate of 71.2% contrasted to the female rate of 28.2% in California in 1989 (California Workers' Compensation Institute, 1990).

Programs which approach some sort of parity between women and men (e.g., Social Security Disability benefits) are still showing a 33% lower benefit rate for women than men (Mudrick, 1988). The Comprehensive Employment & Training Act (CETA) did approach parity, but was dismantled and then replaced by the Job Training and Partnership Act (JPTA) in the early 1980s. The Women's Action Alliance reports that "creaming" is rampant in this program (Sanders, 1988). Creaming is the practice of giving benefits to slim, white, young, preferably childless, women. These women may indeed need services and benefits, but this means that women of color, older women, or women deemed less "attractive" (e.g., disabled, fat) are then denied benefits. Women with children have also lost benefits and services because their childcare expenses are considered too high.

Overall, fewer than 5% of women who need JPTA receive it (Sanders, 1988). Women's groups regard JPTA as a reversal of the trend started in the 1970s with CETA.

The trend started by the 1967 WIN Program was expanded in The Family Services Act (FSA) of 1988 which overhauled the AFDC system and mandated a national workfare program for AFDC recipients known as JOBS. States implementing the program have their own names for it (e.g., in California it is known as GAIN). These programs require women to participate when the youngest child reaches two years of age or risk the loss of AFDC benefits (Fearn, 1990). Many vocational programs designate special needs populations. Within JOBS and the Carl D. Perkins Act of 1984 (renewed in 1990), displaced homemakers, single parents, and teenage mothers are such populations (Reis, 1991). Abuse survivors are represented in these populations and at least one JOBS coordinator estimates levels at 70% in her program (B. Burton, personal communication, November 1, 1990). Indeed, the battered women's movement could be seen as a funnel for many women's entries into the welfare system, and thereby into the newly mandated work programs. Abuse survivors are not recognized as having any special needs in dealing with welfare-mandated workfare programs.

The injuries of domestic violence survivors are recognized in workers' compensation systems, but not because the survivors may be in need of special services, but because there may be a question about the cause of injury. If the injury was caused by domestic violence, then the insurance carrier providing coverage to an employer has a basis for disallowing the claim. The employer or insurance company is obligated to compensate for on-the-job injuries only (Lasky, 1988).

On-the-job rape or sexual harassment survivors are rarely seen in workers' compensation systems since employment discrimination law takes precedence over workers' compensation law. So far, assisting sexual harassment survivors to return to suitable gainful employment by providing vocational rehabilitation benefits and services within employment law systems is an idea whose time has not yet come (Continuing Education of the Bar, 1990).

Although California implemented the provision of vocational expert witness testimony into its dissolution of
marriage code in 1982, the no-fault divorce process has
effectively excluded the battered/raped wife from compensation for her injuries within the divorce process. It is
unclear as to whether or not vocational experts can address
vocational impairment brought about by marital battering
and/or rape inside this 1982 code (California Civil Code
4801, 1992). At the very least, the vocational impairment
which may have resulted from the wife's absence from the
waged labor market because of her homemaking and child
care duties can now be addressed by vocational experts.

---

*...the no-fault divorce process
has effectively excluded the
battered/raped wife from
compensation for her injuries
within the divorce process.*

The emergence of domestic tort law, however, means
that battered/raped wives may sue for damages outside of
the divorce process, but testimony by vocational experts
regarding vocational impairment resulting from abuse is
still rarely seen (Karp & Karp, 1989). This is also true in civil
suits brought on the behalf of sexual assault survivors
(Minnesota Institute of Legal Education, 1990; Institute for
the Study of Sexual Assault, 1983-1987).

I take MacKinnon's (1987) position: "The question then
becomes not whether one trusts the law to behave in a
feminist way. We do not trust medicine, yet we insist it
respond to women's needs. We do not trust theology, but we
claim spirituality as more than a male preserve...If women
are to restrict our demands for change to spheres we can
trust, spheres we already control, there will not be any "(p. 228).
Similarly, I do not expect the vocational rehabilitation profession and the disciplines from which it arises (economics,

law, medicine, education, psychology) to respond to women's needs without the demand, the insistence that women's needs in the various vocational rehabilitation delivery systems first be identified and then acted upon.

In my search for a feminist vocational rehabilitation model, I have come to realize that all current models are based on the work lives of men. For example, Appendix 4 (National Association of Rehabilitation Professionals in the Private Sector [NARPPS] 1989/1990), presents a model for minimal care standards to be offered to clients by vocational rehabilitation practitioners. Nowhere is the reality of women's unwaged work lives as childcare, elder care, and/or housework providers addressed. Other deficiencies in the model are more subtle and not easily located until the model is applied to the reality of violence in women's waged and unwaged work lives.

In my search for a feminist vocational rehabilitation model for women survivors of abuse, I remain true to the origins of my profession.

I chose not to draw from the welfare-related work programs to locate a model for the vocational rehabilitation of women even though these programs do make some attempt to provide for childcare needs as women move into the waged work world. While the masculinist origins of the vocational rehabilitation profession deny and discount the reality of women's work lives, the welfare-related work programs are not structured to acknowledge or handle the reality of injury in women's lives, particularly injuries brought about by rape, battering, and childhood assaults, both physical and sexual. This is not to say that the vocational rehabilitation profession appreciates the nuances of the cycle of violence or the Rape Trauma Syndrome, however, the profession was created to respond to vocational impairments brought about by physical and psychological injuries (Coudroglou & Poole, 1984, pp.13-34). The mix of Byzantine bureaucracy, women's invisible and devalued work identity, and the masculinist origins of the vocational rehabilitation profession has meant that the profession's attention has turned only grudgingly toward the needs of women with an impaired ability to function in the paid labor market. Women's impaired ability to function in the unpaid work world is rarely, if ever, addressed. Therefore, I am not suggesting vocational rehabilitation as any sort of panacea. It's not. In fact, there has never been a vocational rehabilitation program designed specifically for women, and to the best of my knowledge, there are no vocational rehabilitation programs which designate the woman abuse survivor as a special needs client.

In my search for a feminist vocational rehabilitation model for women survivors of abuse, I remain true to the origins of my profession. Ironically, this new model rises out of war just as the masculinist model did. It rises out of that most ancient and unique of wars which has only one name, unlike the internecine patriarchal wars with their many names: the Gulf War, the Civil War, the Trojan War. The name of this war is the Sex War.

I thought I was going to die. I remember saying to God, "Now? And like this?"

—from *Sandra's Story*

sandra's story*

I'm 37 years old, white, from a German Catholic
family. I'm also the adult child of an alcoholic. My
father's the alcoholic and I'm the second child of six,
and the oldest daughter. I'm not sure about my
father's occupation. I know he was in sales, and
when I left home at 18 his job role changed...I guess
I don't really know what his job was. My mother
stayed at home. They both graduated from high
school, but that's it.

I can remember being in kindergarten, getting
hit. Getting hit by my mother and my father. From the
outside, we were the perfect little Catholic family.
We all went to private schools and we all had, you
know, the clothes, the food. When I was five, she hit
me on the left arm with a belt. I was in the kitchen with
her, and I knew Daddy wasn't coming home... there
were other women. The scar was there for such a long
time, maybe 30 years. It must have been the buckle.
The blood coming out—and now it's gone. My father
just hit us with a strap. They didn't hit each other, so
they hit us instead. When I was 10, he went for me
because I yelled, "I hope the new baby dies." I
didn't want the burden of another baby. He went for
me but mother got in the way. She ended up with a
black eye. He was always after me.

I was a straight-A student, but it wasn't good
enough. Once my mother pulled me out of gym class
to tell the nuns I wasn't obeying at home. I know I was
sitting there with the guidance counselor and my
mother while they talked about me, but I wasn't
there. I left. Do you know what I mean? I think I've
always had this artist's soul. I've just never allowed her
to come out. I think she was killed when I was in
kindergarten.

I wanted so many things. I wanted my art but
when I even think about it, I feel my heart being
punctured. I had talent but I didn't know it. If you

---

*In her own words.

don't get feedback, you're invisible. I remember
wishing that someone would recognize me, see me,
discover me. I had a huge secret. I was being hurt at
home. My happy family was a lie, and I was president
of student council. Such conflict. I got sick a lot, that's
how I handled it.

Despite it all, I was drawing for my friends. They
brought me photographs or little pictures and I would
draw them. Some people had collections of my
drawings. One day a nun came up to me and said,
"So what! You're just copying. That's not anything."
I never drew for my friends again.

I worked, too. In high school, I worked in the
cafeteria of a local college. When I graduated, I left
home and got my own apartment. It was 1971 and
I earned $50.00 per week working full-time for the
March of Dimes. Clerical work. I also worked part-
time in a hospital where I rented out televisions to
patients. I wanted so much. I wanted to go away to
college but my friends went away. I lost my best
friend, my haven. She was the source of my self-
esteem. I wanted to go to the private art college in
my city, but my family wanted me to become a
secretary and marry a rich lawyer. But I went to a
local public college and I lived alone and I worked
at a new job as a dispatcher for a crisis counseling
agency. I went to school during the day and I worked
at the agency from four in the afternoon to midnight.
I learned that I didn't want to be a social worker or a
counselor. I learned that counselors are not gods,
some of them were pretty crazy. This would be key
later, after I was assaulted, because I knew better
than to trust counselors.

I graduated from college with a degree in mass
communications and environmental design. Yes, I
am the first person in my family to graduate from
college, but I didn't celebrate this with my family
because every time I shared my dreams with them,
they ignored me. Oh, my brother went to college,
too. My parents supported him.

Then I went to Georgia. Got into my little car and
drove to Georgia where it was warm and where a
friend said there was a good graduate program in
environmental design. I found out that I wanted to
teach. I taught two classes as a graduate assistant

and students came back to me later saying they'd been admitted to Harvard. So I knew I was good. I wished I could have gone to Harvard. I worked, of course. I cleaned houses for a maid service and I was a hostess in a restaurant. Another one of those afternoon to midnight jobs.

Then I graduated and there was an opportunity for me with a guy who was buying houses, remodeling them, and turning them over. We were planning to work together. I would do the designs and the house painting. I was so excited. I looked forward to the combination of physical labor and the artistic part of it.

Then, in a split second, my life changed. I had just bought a puppy, and I went to the vet's to pick him up after his shots. Only the attendant was there. As I turned to go out the door he said, "Get back in that room." He locked the door. I left my body the moment he said that. I thought I was going to die. I remember saying to God, "Now? And like this?" I couldn't believe it. I was so happy. I had just finished my degree. I had new and exciting work. I didn't drink. I didn't do drugs. I didn't go out on dates. I was a good girl. He kept me there for five hours. While he told me his story, I became his friend. He was a Vietnam vet and he didn't know who he was. I was terrorized but I couldn't show him because he liked my fear. I could see that. I wasn't figuring all this out, you know. It's amazing how you do what you do—just to live. He reminded me of a man I had known and so I told him about my friend. It wasn't a lie. It all came from my heart to him. He didn't penetrate me. He didn't physically injure me. The scars are all on the inside. I made him feel safe, and so he let me go. He said, "Maybe we can go to dinner sometime." I don't remember how I got home. I drove because my car was outside my door. I was able to call a friend back home, and then I didn't move for a long, long time. Days passed. I don't know where they went. I did go back the next day though because my dog was still there. Can you imagine? I went back. I was afraid he would kill my dog. I had to go back.

Then I gave up my dog. I gave up my new job. I cut off my waist-length hair. I never wore any clothes that were tight. I also numbed myself below the waist. I've just learned that if I don't have strong legs, strong pelvis then I don't have to be sexual. I moved to an island into a room with one door. I lived there for five years, and when I left I realized that I had never once opened the blinds. I also don't remember eating the whole time I was there. I didn't tell my family for more than seven years and they still couldn't handle it or me. I did work as a house painter because I could be alone. I worked and worked and worked.

The rapist? My friends talked me into reporting it. I did it for the other women he might be raping. That got to me. I didn't do it for me. They put him in jail and there was a trial. I had no medical treatment. I had no counseling. I was not referred to a rape crisis center. I had no explanations of any of the legal procedures-depositions, grand jury hearings, or the trial. One policeman said to me, "Well, you were lucky he didn't cut you up."

Turns out the guy was on parole for doing this to other women or they wouldn't have picked him up at all. Turns out he had kids. He was married. He cried on the witness stand. They let him go. He got off. That's when I moved to the island. You see, it must have been something I did. They let him go, so I must be guilty. If he's not guilty, then I must be.

In 1985, the criminal investigator on the case knocked on my door. She told me he was back in jail for another rape and this time it was for keeps. Then I could say, "See! He was guilty. It wasn't me." I count this as the start of my recovery. When they let him out, I went in. Now that he was back in jail, I could get out. I left the island and I moved north to the mountains. I'm doing movement therapy and I'm having dreams which surprised me. It's been 10 years and I'm just now having dreams about it? My movement therapist says it's reawakening, and that it's okay. I've never gone back to design. I mean what am I supposed to say when someone asks: "What have you been doing for the past 10 years?"

I volunteer at the rape crisis center. I work in a bakery and as a waitress. I have friends. I can go out and have dinner and remember eating. I would like to make a video about the psychology of space. Maybe consult with law firms, courts of law, hotels on how rape survivors need safe and beautiful rooms.

three

post-traumatic stress disorder and abuse survivors

About 80% of women in prostitution have been the victim of a rape, and it's kind of hard to talk about this because....the experience of prostitution is just like rape. You have to imagine it. You have to think of it as they experience it. Here you are alone in a room and here's the money. And then he gets to take you. He gets to put his fist, his boot, or his snake, or his gun, or his knife, or his penis, or anything he wants to in any orifice of your body for as long and as hard as he wants to **because he bought the right to do it.** *That and that alone is the experience of prostitution....This rape is not that....this is the rape of any woman. Prostitutes are raped, on the average, eight to ten times per year. They are, I believe, the most raped class of women in the history of our planet.* (Hunter & Reed, 1990)

That's the sky and that's a leaf and he shoves his penis in my mouth. I die looking at the sky and he pushes and shoves and it feels like the roof of my mouth has to split open soon. And it feels like he's all the way down my throat. I can't breathe! I need to throw up! WHERE is the sky? WHERE is the leaf? I can't see anything. I'm going

*to be sick. I want to DIE. I leave my body. I hide in my
forehead and then in the sky." (Strong, 1988, pp. 84-85)*

---

*One had a six-centimeter gash ripped in her vagina by
a husband who was trying to "pull her vagina out."*
(Finkelhor & Yllo, 1985, p. 18)

---

*Indeed, their [rape victims] level of PTSD, as assessed
by the IES, is equal to that of the combat veterans....*
(Wilson, Smith, & Johnson, 1985, pp. 142)

---

*Women represent 55% of all stress claimants in Califor-
nia, double the percentage of women experiencing
disabling work injuries.* (California Workers' Compensation Institute, 1990)

The Korean War, the Vietnam War, and the heightened
awareness of the Sex War (brought about by the women's
movement of the 1960s and 1970s) resulted in a still-ex-
panding synergistic analysis of trauma and its consequences.
I am not the first person to notice that the injuries of abuse
survivors and combat veterans are similar. Indeed, the
emerging data on post-traumatic stress disorder (PTSD)
emphasizes the commonalities among a wide variety of
survivor groups including combat veterans, rape survivors,
battered women, childhood sexual assault survivors, holocaust survivors, industrially injured workers, and survivors
of natural disasters (Figley, 1985). The inclusion of the
PTSD diagnosis into the *Diagnostic and Statistical Manual
of Mental Disorders (DSM-III)* in 1980 (and its maintenance
in subsequent revisions as in the *DSM-III-R*) offers an ex-
traordinary opportunity for rehabilitationists to provide
services to abuse survivors within the hodgepodge of rehabilitation delivery systems (American Psychiatric Association, 1987). We now have a psychological diagnosis which
refutes Freud's (1966) assertion that "almost all my women

patients told me that they had been seduced by their fathers. I was driven to recognize in the end that these reports were untrue and so came to understand that the hysterical symptoms are derived from phantasies and not from real occurrences (p. 584)."

The abandonment of the abuse survivor by the disciplines of psychology and psychiatry was not corrected until the rise of the second wave of the women's movement in the United States in the 1960s and 1970s.

There is a masculinist history of trauma as neurosis which dates back to the seventeenth and eighteenth centuries. The nineteenth century is, of course, marked by the emergence of Freud and the Freudian school (Trimble, 1985). Freud and his followers effectively solidified the rape paradigm concept that women lie about abuse experiences. In comparison, Freud was quick to recognize trauma suffered by combat veterans (Trimble, 1985). The abandonment of the abuse survivor by the disciplines of psychology and psychiatry was not corrected until the rise of the second wave of the women's movement in the United States in the 1960s and 1970s (Meiselman, 1984; Rush, 1980). The return of combat veterans from Korea, and particularly Vietnam, brought the long-term effects of trauma on survivors to the attention of the public and the helping professions (Trimble, 1985). By 1985, journal articles reflected comparative analyses of survivor groups which included combat veterans and rape survivors (Wilson et al., 1985).

This development is valuable because it not only provides a more dignified psychological diagnosis to the abuse survivor, since it is more reflective of her experience, but also because it meets the Frye test in legal systems (as a diagnosis recognized by experts in the field) (Kennedy, 1983). It also provides a diagnosis which will meet eligibility requirements for the provision of rehabilitation services and benefits in the various delivery systems (e.g., Social Security Disability, state departments of rehabilitation). Previous psychological diagnoses have been regarded as insulting by abuse survivors who do not regard themselves as schizophrenic, hysterical, manic-depressive (bi-polar), or crazy (N. Hamel, personal communication, January 16, 1989). The dignity of survivors may also be undermined by racism and it is important to note that as powerful a tool as the PTSD diagnosis might be, white women's responses to trauma cannot be taken as the norm.

The experience of PTSD has its cultural and ethnic foundations. "Ethnic identification is an irreducible entity, central to how persons organize experience, and to an understanding of the unique cultural prism they use in perception and evaluation of reality (Parson, 1985, p. 315)." Parson provides an example of a Puerto Rican woman who had been raped and then diagnosed by the treating physician as having a "physically violent dissociative episode (1985, p. 333)." This diagnosis may have re-victimized the rape survivor, which possibly could have been avoided if the physician had acknowledged "that the patient had undergone a culturally accepted manner of expressing stress and conflict called *ataques* (p. 334)."

Therefore, the PTSD diagnosis is a tool to be used with caution. The complexities of trauma and the human response to it should not be underestimated. For example, is post-traumatic stress disorder a psychological response only? Apparently not, because recent studies indicate that "a single instance of overwhelming terror can alter the chemistry of the brain, making people more sensitive to adrenaline surges even decades later (Goleman, 1990, pp. B5, B9)."

An approach to the use of the PTSD diagnosis may lie in the "whole person" concept which was codified into Oregon workers' compensation law in an apparent effort to avoid the Kafkaesque grotesqueries brought about by physicians writing medical reports which document injury ratings to different parts of the same person's body, as though an injury in one part of the body does not influence the whole body, mind and soul, or in short, the whole person (Bruyere, S., 1986; B. M. Karls, personal communication, June 10, 1991). Therefore, although I have separated psychological injuries of abuse survivors from their physical injuries, this division should be regarded as arbitrary and of no use in dealing with a living, breathing human being.

When the impact of one rape experience and the resulting PTSD in a nonprostituted woman such as Sandra is understood, the trauma experienced by the continual rape of women used in prostitution can hardly be imagined.

I am not suggesting that all abuse survivors suffer from PTSD, but that the PTSD diagnosis gives rehabilitationists a tool we have not had in this century until 1980. The focus of this chapter, then, is not to explore all psychological injuries which result from abuse since that would be beyond the scope of this book. For example, Multiple Personality Disorder (MPD), which is placed within the Dissociative Disorders in the *DSM-III-R*, is an important diagnosis for abuse survivors since populations with this disorder have usually suffered from extraordinarily violent and prolonged abuse experiences (American Psychiatric Association, 1987). The Council for Prostitution Alternatives (CPA) estimates that approximately 15% of the prostitution survivors using their agency suffer from MPD. Counselors trained in MPD dynamics are on the staff of this agency (S.K. Hunter, personal communication, December 30, 1990).

Sandra's Story is the story of a rape survivor with PTSD. (The diagnostic criteria for PTSD from the *DSM-III-R* are reprinted in Table 2.) Sandra experienced "an event outside the range of usual human experience." Ten years after the assault, Sandra is now having "recurrent distressing dreams of the event." Perhaps the most dramatic illustration of PTSD in *Sandra's Story* is her "efforts to avoid thoughts and feelings associated with the trauma, inability to recall an important aspect of the trauma, feeling of detachment or estrangement from others." Sandra shared this response with every other co-researcher in this book, and her inability to remember is a constant theme in all of the co-researcher's stories. The numbing of her body, particularly the pelvic region, is a good reminder of the whole person concept when dealing with PTSD. Although Sandra's hypervigilance eased after her rapist was incarcerated, she is still not able to be fully in the world within her profession. "Difficulty in concentrating" is probably also a barrier to her return to the career goals she held prior to the rape. *Anita's Story* documents the heroic efforts of this survivor to overcome concentration difficulties by taking a course in logic while being battered. Her joy at passing the course, even with a D, becomes understandable when the PTSD diagnostic criteria are applied. When the impact of one rape experience and the resulting PTSD in a nonprostituted woman such as Sandra is understood, the trauma experienced by the continual rape of women used in prostitution can hardly be imagined. There is no journal article on PTSD in the prostitution survivor population. However, the PTSD studies of holocaust survivors and their children may offer some clues. The abstract from "The Treatment and Prevention of Long-term Effects and Intergenerational Transmission of Victimization: A Lesson From Holocaust Survivors and Their Children (Daniele, 1985)," provides both a cautionary and instructive approach to examining PTSD in the prostitution survivor population:

The heterogeneity of responses of families of survivors to their Holocaust (prostitution) and post-Holocaust (prostitution survivor) life experiences, described within and beyond the current notions of post-traumatic stress disorder, emphasizes the need to guard against expecting all victim-survivors to behave in a uniform fashion and to match appropriate therapeutic interventions to particular forms of reaction. The discussion delineates the meanings of the victimization rupture, preventive and reparative goals, and principles and modalities of treatment (professional and self-help) of the long-term effects and intergenerational transmission of the traumata. Highly needed training, which is traditionally absent, should include working through therapists' "countertransference" difficulties. (p. 295)

When we consider Hunter and Reed's (1990) description of the prostitution experience combined with rape above and beyond that eight to ten times per year, as well as kidnapping, torture, battery, suicide attempts, fear of murder, and no resources (e.g., access to education, jobs, stable housing and income, child care) examining holocaust studies for an understanding of prostitution survivors does not appear to be inappropriate (Neland, undated). The re-victimization of this class of women is comparable to that of holocaust victims. *Sandra's Story* is the story of one rape experience, but her trauma continues after 10 years. A prostitution survivor who has been used in prostitution for the CPA's average of eight years may equal or exceed the years spent in concentration camps by holocaust victims (Neland, undated). Hunter estimates that some prostitution survivors need as many as 10 years of active recovery work (personal communication, December 30, 1990).

Substance abuse disorders are common complications of PTSD and 85% of the CPA prostitution survivors suffer from drug and alcohol addiction (Neland, undated). Prostitution is apparently not possible to endure without some sort of chemical numbing (Giobbe, 1990).

Table 2

Diagnostic Criteria for 309.89 Post-traumatic Stress Disorder

A. The person has experienced an event that is outside the range of usual human experience and that would be markedly distressing to almost anyone, e.g., serious threat to one's life or physical integrity; serious threat or harm to one's children, spouse, or other close relatives and friends; sudden destruction of one's home or community; or seeing another person who has recently been, or is being, seriously injured or killed as the result of an accident or physical violence.

B. The traumatic event is persistently reexperienced in at least one of the following ways:

1. recurrent and intrusive distressing recollections of the event (in young children, repetitive play in which themes or aspects of the trauma are expressed)
2. recurrent distressing dreams of the event
3. sudden acting or feeling as if the traumatic event were recurring (includes a sense of reliving the experience, illusions, hallucinations, and dissociative [flashback] episodes, even those that occur upon awakening or when intoxicated)
4. intense psychological distress at exposure to events that symbolize or resemble an aspect of the traumatic event, including anniversaries of the trauma

Reprinted with permission from the *Diagnostic and Statistical Manual of Mental Disorders (Third Edition-Revised): DSM-III-R*, Washington, D.C.: American Psychiatric Association, 1987. p. 247-251.

(Continued on next page)

Chapter Three

C. Persistent avoidance of stimuli associated with the trauma or numbing of general responsiveness (not present before the trauma), as indicated by at least three of the following:

   1. efforts to avoid thoughts or feelings associated with the trauma
   2. efforts to avoid activities or situations that arouse recollections of the trauma
   3. inability to recall an important aspect of the trauma (psychogenic amnesia)
   4. markedly diminished interest in significant activities (in young children, loss of recently acquired developmental skills such as toilet training or language skills)
   5. feeling of detachment or estrangement from others
   6. restricted range of affect, e.g., unable to have loving feelings
   7. sense of a foreshortened future, e.g., does not expect to have a career, marriage, or children, or a long life.

D. Persistent symptoms of increased arousal (not present before the trauma), as indicated by at least two of the following:

   1. difficulty falling or staying asleep
   2. irritability or outbursts of anger
   3. difficulty concentrating
   4. hypervigilance
   5. exaggerated startle response
   6 physiologic reactivity upon exposure to events that symbolize or resemble an aspect of the traumatic event (e.g., a woman who was raped in an elevator breaks out in a sweat when entering any elevator)

E. Duration of the disturbance (symptoms in B, C, and D) of at least one month.

Specify delayed onset if the onset of symptoms was at least six months after the trauma.

The issue of substance abuse leads to a "chicken and egg go-around" in that substance abuse can lead to prostitution as a means of supporting a drug habit, and prostitution demands chemical numbing in order to endure it. Perhaps one of the more startling developments in CPA's understanding of the prostitution survivor is recognizing that 10% to 15% of the survivors are victims of Fetal Alcohol Syndrome (FAS) or Fetal Alcohol Effect (FAE). That is, these are the daughters of mothers who abused alcohol during pregnancy. Some of these mothers were prostitutes. Others were most likely victims also using alcohol to manage the trauma of battering, rape, and incest (American Psychiatric Association, 1987). Both FAS and FAE have physical and mental effects resulting in mental retardation, delayed language development, school problems, difficulty in relationships, growth deficiencies, facial abnormalities, malformations of various organ systems and external genitalia, as well as limited joint movements of fingers and elbows (Doweiko, 1990). FAE is a milder, less symptomatic manifestation of FAS. We have not yet begun to see cocaine babies as adults. If we do not end prostitution, we can expect these daughters (who survive) to also emerge within this class of women.

The data from CPA point out how putting prostitution at the center of the rape paradigm allows for a multilayered and far-reaching examination of abuse dynamics and their consequences. These particular data demand a reexamination of the woman's right to choose/fetal rights issue in terms of violence against women. Treating women with substance abuse problems (alcohol or drugs or both) cannot be based on a male treatment model because violence against women is not taken into account. *Anita's Story* provides a good example of the failure of current treatment models: *People said I was co-dependent. I was able to understand some of it, but it didn't work. I would walk out of the room. Then I'm locking myself into a room. Then why is he breaking down the door? Why isn't this Al-Anon stuff working?*

FAS and FAE are described as the only potentially preventable major birth defects, but this prevention will never occur without stopping violence against women, without stopping the use of women in systems of prostitution (Doweiko, 1990).

Rehabilitationists working in agencies providing services to the mentally retarded and developmentally disabled will recognize the FAS and FAE population as part of their client population. But what they may not recognize is the vulnerability of this population to assault and to enslavement inside systems of prostitution. Rehabilitationists need to regard clients diagnosed with FAE or FAS as not only from families with alcoholism histories but also with possible abuse histories as well. The intergenerational transmission of abuse is now well documented (Herrenkohl, Herrenkohl, & Toedter, 1983). And the connections between incest or family sexual abuse and a life of prostitution continue to surface over and over in data on prostitution survivor populations (Neland, undated). Therefore, a rehabilitationist attempting to serve the FAE and FAS client population without an understanding of abuse issues and the interconnections among alcohol, substance abuse, and PTSD cannot be providing quality services.

Battered Woman Syndrome (BWS) and Rape Trauma Syndrome (RTS) are considered to be subcategories of PTSD (Campbell, 1990; Massaro, 1985). Both BWS and RTS concepts can be applied to the prostitution survivor. There is also new research documenting PTSD in incest survivors (Donaldson & Gardner, 1985). However, the current state of ignorance regarding the damage caused by the prostitution experience will require that we use the information developed through research and clinical experiences with other PTSD survivor groups until more sophisticated data emerge. CPA's data base of more than 800 prostitution survivors gives rehabilitationists a start (Neland, undated). I do not mean to suggest that there is no connection between the experiences of rape, battering, and incest for prostitution survivors and other women, thereby supporting the weird (but common) notion that prostitutes are not human or are not women (Wiegan, 1990). My intent is to point out that the concept of prostitution as violence against women, is still poorly understood and the task is to make all of the connections between the prostitution experience and all the forms of woman abuse.

In summary, the PTSD diagnosis is a powerful tool which must be used by rehabilitationists with care. Racist insensitivity to an abuse survivor may result in her re-victimization. Lack of knowledge regarding the connections between substance abuse, violence against women and PTSD may result in inadequate provision of services. The lack of research on PTSD in the prostitution survivor population does not imply that prostitutes do not experience trauma. The data now available on battered women, rape survivors, and sexually assaulted children indicate high levels of trauma. Since prostitutes are also battered women, rape survivors, and sexually assaulted children, their trauma levels at least equal if not exceed that of nonprostituted women.

She got herself out of the trap and away from the giant, and out of the dungeon. Jesus Christ! Yeah! I always thought of it as running away. I never thought of it as strength.

–from *Mary's Story*

mary's story*

Can I have a handkerchief? This might be tough. It's not easy to talk about this. It's taboo especially in the workplace where I've been a social worker, now a therapist, now a doctoral student. It was important for me to appear invincible. It's a way of being invisible to yourself, ultimately.

Yesterday was Mother's Day and I think of the children in my life and I try to ignore it because I deliberately did not have children because of my abuse history. I'm 42 years old now and I was raised in Orange County in Southern California. I have a younger sister. We are a white family with no particular religious background. I was raised by my mother and father—periodically. My mother was mentally ill. She was in and out of hospitals while I was growing up. She was diagnosed as bipolar or manic-depressive.

When I was two years old I remember something had happened which made her feel bad. She was nude. She was running around the house without clothes and then she picked me up and threw me into the bathtub. She held me down...and the water... I remember she was crying and she held me under water. I was the only one there. I don't know where my father was, but then, just like that, she passed out. Oh shit! I'm having body memories of this occurrence right now. Running out of the house, down the street, on the grass, and the flagstones on the porch. My God! Whew! That little girl knew something was happening, and she managed to get out of the tub, and she was all wet. She got herself out of the trap and away from the giant, and out of the dungeon. Jesus Christ! Yeah! I always thought of it as running away. I never thought of it as strength.

I think I can go on now.

My mother and father were very sexual, not in love, but sexual. It kept them together because they

---

*In her own words.

hated each other. They fought constantly. My father hit my mother. I saw him do it. He sent her to the hospital twice.

When I was seven, and for some damn reason, that was the watershed year for pure, unadulterated hell. I was abused by both my mother and my father and I was forbidden to see my grandmother and my grandfather. Then there was this teacher at school. I had always been fascinated by sex, how animals had sex, how people had sex, anatomy, physiology. I found an anatomy chart and it showed the cross-section of a woman. You know, the cervix, the large colon, the bladder. I was looking at the different parts and the teacher made me stay after class. She grabbed my arms and dug her fingernails into me. Standing over me she said, "Where did you get that? Where did you get that?" I didn't tell her because I couldn't remember. She was hurting me and she was allowed to do this because my parents always believed everything the teachers said about me and I don't understand because I was a good student. What a year. I also started having trouble with the other kids. They teased me. They would gang up on me. I ran away.

At home I wasn't allowed to watch television. I had to practice the piano and my penmanship because the teacher said my writing wasn't legible. I had very little time, and then my mother would come in and kiss me goodnight before bed. I didn't want her to kiss me goodnight. I was mad. I hated her. I think the only thing my parents ever agreed on was that I needed to be controlled.

I think my father wanted me to be a boy. He used to spank me a lot. He used to spank me because I'd be making noise. He hit me in the head with his fist or his open hand in bed at night because I might have been making noise or horsing around or something. "If you don't shut up, I'll give you something to cry about." I remember seeing stars more than once. I was hit maybe five times per week. It was great getting a day off. I would run away to my grandparents' house down the block. My mother would say, "You're a bad child. You're a disobedient child." When I was 11, my mother really flipped out. She started getting real vague. She couldn't make decisions. Her appearance would deteriorate when usually she was a very neat woman. She would laugh inappropriately and talk about sex. She'd say, "Dicks, fucking, pussy." I think she was assaulted by her father. Now she's almost 70 years old and she's still afraid to be without a man. But when I was 11 I decided: "Not me. Not me. I don't care what happens to me in life. I'm going to be able to take care of myself, at least economically." And so what's happened is that I make relationships with men who don't have economic power over me. Sometimes I feel like I'm buying sex from the men in my life because I've ended up supporting them. I don't like that. I feel that I can't have both, a relationship with a man and economic independence. I feel as though I'm being punished for being smart or having a career. It's just not fair.

I went to live with my grandparents when I was 11. My parents had a terrible custody battle over me and my sister. I lived with my grandparents until I was 17. My sister was raised by my mother after she got out of the hospital. These were the best years of my life. I finally gained some social skills. My grandparents loved me. I went to a new school and I lived to learn. My father would come around and boss me. My mother would do strange things like give me a leopard skin negligee for my 16th birthday.

I left for college when I was 17 and got married when I was 18. I think I was legitimizing a sexual relationship because, at the time, you couldn't get birth control without permission from an adult. My grandmother had to sign a note for me to get birth control pills. He was my high school sweetheart. He went to Vietnam and I went to college. When he came back our relationship deteriorated, and we divorced. There was no violence. He wouldn't communicate.

I then went on to work as an eligibility worker while attending college to get my bachelor's degree in social work. I paid for my own education.

I started dating, and went out with this guy who took me back to his place which he shared with this horrible old man who watched when my so-called date raped me. I let him have sex with me rather than put up a fuss. I was afraid of being hurt. Then the old man fell asleep and my date fell asleep. Six months after this experience I got a letter from this sicko telling me how screwed up I was. I was so upset I moved from my apartment so that he couldn't find me. I tried to tell my grandmother but she disappointed me by telling me that I should never have gone out with him. I have been in a rape support group for this problem, so it's pretty well resolved.

My second important man, Joe, and I would have violent arguments. I had moved to Flagstaff, Arizona with him for my asthma which I had developed after graduating from college. I seem to have a tolerance for abuse. I let things just go on, and on...even at work where I let a woman, who was an ex-Air Force nurse, intimidate me. She finally got me fired. Joe didn't have a job and I was very angry about that. We'd go around and around. Both work and home were horrible. I'd incite my Joe by name-calling and then he and I would fight each other physically. Once he threw me out on a porch. He wasn't a very big guy, but strong, fast, and a better fighter than me. Once he dragged me around the block by my arms. I'd go to work with bruises and tell them I had gotten hurt in a car door, that I fell down, that I cut myself in the kitchen. I took a drug overdose two weeks after starting therapy. My first therapist had paid no attention when I told him I was suicidal. I did call a friend though, and I ended up in intensive care. They treated me like dog shit because I had tried to kill myself. I changed therapists, it helped. I did learn to handle work better with assertiveness skills. I wanted children and kept pushing Joe to get married. We split up.

I moved again. I met my second husband. I met him at a neighbor's house. He was an electrician. We were making the same amount of money which was a first for me since I usually choose guys who make less money than me. I went click(!), "Oh boy, the perfect man. Now I can get married and have a baby." That biological clock was really ticking. He turned out to be an alcoholic. I didn't know that alcoholics were people who drank cocktails in the evening until two in the morning and then went to work. I thought alcoholics were people in the gutter.

I got a new job after moving to the Palmdale area where I met Charlie and I continued to have problems with my supervisors. I was accused of unprofessional behaviors. I was outspoken, passive/aggressive. I always felt shame and guilt around any authority figures, uneasy. I felt stigmatized. In my social work, I've had trouble with my bosses. I didn't have assertiveness skills, communication skills. I would do whatever my bosses said. I would never say "no." They would never say "thank you." And then I would resent them and they could feel it. It was like the old days, my old troubles in grade school with the other kids.

The verbal abuse with Charlie started before we were married. The physical stuff started after the marriage. After the separation, I cut my hair very short because he used to drag me around the house with it. He put me into the hospital twice. Once I had a neck injury and the other time I cannot remember the injuries. I still have neck and shoulder problems from that, and migraine headaches. Then I had to have a hysterectomy and basically he was never home after that. He'd be off in a bar somewhere, drinking.

I did have a good job for about five years of the marriage as a county social worker. I pretty much worked on my own. I really liked it, but sometimes Charlie would call me at work and start arguments with me. He came to my office and harassed me when I had clients there. Sometimes, he'd come by a couple of times a day. I think I lost this job because of the battering. I made excuses, of course, about being in the hospital. I said it was an auto accident. Another door story about bruises. Falling down stories. All that. I wasn't paying enough attention at work. I was stressed all the time. I couldn't really give it my best. I couldn't really be there for my clients.

We separated after a wrestling incident with a loaded gun. I got a restraining order. I started going to a battered women's support group. I went back into therapy. I moved again! To work as a social worker, but also to go back to school. Now I'm working on my doctorate in human sexuality. I'm almost done. I'm not recovered, but I'm on the path. I want to write, to do educational consulting, to provide therapy for sexually dysfunctional people. Everyday, I write my affirmations. I meditate. I go to a 12-Step group whenever I can. The Adult Child of Alcoholics rings the biggest bell for me. I feel my recovery in my professional life at last. I have something special to bring to my clients. I can say I've been there. I know what it feels like.

four

---

the physical injuries of abuse survivors

Consider the fact that an estimated 3 to 4 million American women in the United States are battered and assaulted, including rape, each year by their husbands or partners. Many of these women are permanently injured—not just physically, but mentally—while some of them lose their lives. In the aggregate, as many as 15 million women in this country have been abused at some time during their lives, either as children, adolescents or adults. Consider also that each year 1 million women are sufficiently injured to seek medical assistance at emergency rooms for injuries sustained through battering. It's an overwhelming moral, economic, and public health burden that our society can no longer bear. Battery is the single most significant cause of injury to women in this country. Physical injuries of approximately 1 in 5 women seen in hospital emergency rooms were caused by spouse abuse. (Koop, 1990, p. 1)

In 19% of the rape cases, the victims tried to stop the violence by telling the assailant that they were prostitutes....Rather than assuage the violence, this assertion only exacerbated the problem: the assailant increased the amount of violence in every single case....In most of the cases, the victims sustained some physical injury: 69% sustained injuries on the face or body, 38% sustained injuries in the genital area; 13% had broken bones, 22% suffered shock. On the average, in each rape case the victim sustained 2 to 4 different kinds of injuries. (Silbert, 1988, p. 80-81)

Black eyes, bloody noses, cigarette burns, broken bones, all these and more were described to us as injuries inflicted in the course of sexual assault. Another physiological consequence of forced sex was damage to the genitals and rectum. Rough, forceful penetration with inadequate lubrication caused varying degrees of injury, including vaginal soreness, swollen labia, and in some instances, lacerations....a third of the women reported forced anal sex. All of these women described some degree of physical injuries, ranging from soreness to hemorrhoids to torn muscles. (Finkelhor & Yllo, 1985, p. 122)

A woman met a man in a hotel room in the 5th Ward. When she got there she was tied up while sitting on a chair nude. She was gagged and left alone in the dark for what she believed to be an hour. The man returned with two other men. They burned her with cigarettes and attached nipple clamps to her breasts. They had many S and M magazines with them and showed her many pictures of women appearing to consent, enjoy, and encourage this abuse. She was held for 12 hours, continuously raped and beaten. She was paid $50 or about $2.33 per hour. (Dworkin, 1989, p. 316)

The power of denial is like an arctic wind blowing over memory and freezing it so that feelings and facts are lost both to the survivor and to the rehabilitationist who may be providing services. If it's not real to the survivor, how can it be real to me, the helper, who has not had the experience?

The psychic numbing of post-traumatic stress disorder is not confined to emotional and psychological amnesia but to the physical experience of abuse as well (Campbell, 1990). Who can forget the photograph of Hedda Nussbaum's smashed face on the cover of the February 13, 1989 issue of *People Magazine?* Although her injuries included a damaged tear duct, broken jaw, broken nose, broken ribs, ruptured spleen, gangrenous leg, and cauliflower ear, Nussbaum minimized the beatings she received from Joel Steinberg, even after the death of her illegally adopted daughter, Lisa, at Steinberg's hands (Johnson, 1989).

Nussbaum's denial of her own physical injuries is a common trait of battered women, and is one of the characteristics of PTSD, and its subcategory, Battered Woman's Syndrome (BWS) (Johnson, 1989). Another aspect of BWS is the inability to recall an important aspect of the trauma. Mary reports in her story that she cannot recall why she had to go to the emergency room after a beating. She does know that she has neck and upper back pain and migraine headaches from an apparent neck injury as a result of being beaten, but the specific details as to when, how, and even where the injury took place continue to elude her. The details of Mary's physical injuries are so casually tossed into her story they are almost invisible. I selected *Mary's Story* for placement at the front of this chapter for exactly that reason. Mary's recovery story, then, becomes focused on psychological recovery rather than physical recovery. This may be because there is probably little or no further recovery to be expected for Mary's neck and back. As a rehabilitationist, I know that as Mary ages, she will face deterioration in the injured disks. Arthritis in the injured portion of the spine is a common complication. The point is, injuries do not have to be dramatic to produce lifelong disabling effects as well as lifelong physical discomfort and pain.

For survivors of child abuse, both physical and sexual, the blocking of memory may be so complete that the origin of an injury resulting in permanent disability may be completely lost. A ritual abuse survivor advised me privately that it took her more than two years of active recovery work to understand her lifelong mid-back problems. This disabling injury was inflicted upon her at the age of eight, more than 30 years ago, during a sexual assault upon her and her sister by a group.

The contraction of sexually transmitted diseases by sexually abused children is rarely understood by the child, and as an adult, the survivor may discover her abuse only through the process of trying to track down her own health history. One woman in my workers' compensation caseload had contracted herpes. At the age of 10 she was taken to the doctor for treatment. The doctor humiliated her by scolding her for "being with the boys." She had no idea what he was talking about since she could not recall her abuse. The survivor now understands that she contracted herpes as a result of sexual abuse starting at the age of four.

A ritual abuse survivor advised me privately that it took her more than two years of active recovery work to understand her lifelong mid-back problems.

The minimizing or the forgetting of physical injury also includes denial of physical pain. Marlene tells us in her story: *Actually, it's hard for me to make sense about something being painful. I have a difficult time paying attention to pain even now.* She then goes on to report how her inability to acknowledge the signals her body sends her has exacerbated an injury to her shoulder. She will now require surgery which she may have avoided had she been able to listen to her body's pain.

While interviewing one of the co-researchers, I discovered that she had recently experienced a back injury at work as the result of a fall. She had to be prodded, by me, into a more active stance in the management of her own medical care. When I asked her later why this was so, she replied, "When I was being battered, I was in so much pain I just lived with it." She also reported that her treating physician was horrified at the pain levels she was enduring without any assistance whatsoever (e.g., drugs, physical therapy). We concluded that continued abuse results in a denial of one of the body's important defense mechanisms–pain.

For some women, the denial of pain and injury may be one of the few tactics available to manage pain and injury, however badly. Many battered women, prostitutes battered by pimps or johns, rape survivors, and children do not have the resources (e.g., money, transportation) which would allow them access to medical care. Shelter workers advise me that women with obvious physical injuries are dependent on overburdened free clinics, publicly funded emergency rooms, or the rare volunteer nurses and physicians (N. Hamel, personal communication, December 19, 1990; Ehrlich, 1989). Shelter workers also report a desperate need for dental care, including oral surgery. Missing and fractured teeth, and lacerated gums are commonly found injuries in shelter populations. Battered children, who accompany their battered mothers into the shelter, have similar injuries. Locating free or low-cost dental care is extremely difficult.

Then there's the problem of identifying injuries to the genitals which are hidden by shame and privacy. This is reflected in *Anita's Story*, where she points out: *In my survivor's group, we didn't tap into sexual abuse....It's still not talked about, even within the battered women's movement.* And yet many of stories in this book have some mention of injury or disease affecting the pelvis or genitals. The list is as follows: venereal disease and sterilization–*Laura's Story;* numbing below the waist–*Sandra's Story;* hysterectomy–*Mary's Story;* pain in the lower back/pelvic area–*Miranda's Story;* rape–*Liz's Story;* forcible penile penetration after cervical surgery–*Harriet's Story;* yeast infections and IUD perforation of the uterus–*Marlene's Story;* hints of assault and injury to genitals–*Anita's Story.* Perhaps the most elusive and perplexing of injuries in the abuse survivor populations are traumatic head injuries. It has only been within the last 10 years that specialized head injury treatment programs have been available to the general population (Fanning,

1990). And although beatings can certainly cause traumatic head injuries, survivors may never get a diagnosis of head injury, but instead be regarded as mentally ill or retarded. The National Head Injury Foundation (Deutsch & Fralish, 1990) defines traumatic brain injury as:

> An insult to the brain, not of a degenerative or congenital nature but caused by an external force, that may produce a diminished or altered state of consciousness, which results in impairment of cognitive abilities or physical functioning. It can also result in disturbance of behavioral or emotional functioning. These impairments may be either temporary or permanent and cause partial or total functional disability or psychosocial maladjustment. (p. xiv)

Physical problems resulting from traumatic head injury are the most easily identified and may include an inability to ambulate or to speak normally. More subtle physical problems can include visual deficits such as double vision. Fine motor skills may be impaired due to tremors or poor coordination (Deutsch & Fralish, 1990).

Cognitive difficulties can include concentration–attention problems; short- and long-term memory deficits; an inability to abstract or generalize, which is essential to problem solving; poor organization and planning; erratic processing speed, either too slow or too rapid (Deutsch & Fralish, 1990).

A look at the PTSD characteristics reprinted as Table 2 lists "difficulty in concentrating" as one of the criteria for a diagnosis of PTSD. Behavioral characteristics of the traumatically head-injured include impulsivity and socially inappropriate behaviors, which may also be difficult to distinguish from the PTSD criterion of "irritability or outbursts of anger," or "exaggerated startle response." A careful comparison between the PTSD diagnosis and 310.2 Postconcussional Syndrome on page 473 of the *DSM-III-R* (American Psychiatric Association, 1987) is strongly recommended by a staff psychologist with the Division of Corrections in Maryland. He sees head-injured people diagnosed with everything from schizophrenia to antisocial behavior (Despres, 1990). Adding to the complexity of the problem is that "unlike people with other disabilities, individuals with head injury are characterized more by their differences than by their similarities. No two people who turn to the rehabilitation specialist for treatment are the same. Thus, all require individualized programs that specifically address the strengths and limitations exhibited by that person (Deutsch & Fralish, 1990, pp. 1-1- 1.03[4])."

This oversight may lead to serious problems for survivors who are caught up in a rehabilitationist's desire to provide family intervention services without knowing that the survivor may be risking her life by returning to the family where her injury was inflicted!

Deutsch and Fralish (1990) also point out that "one of the most unique features of head injury rehabilitation is the relative lack of territorial battles between professional disciplines....and is most likely attributable to a realization that no one discipline and no one professional had the answers to the perplexing questions raised by traumatic head injury" (p. xiii). Despite this optimistic attitude, these authors have overlooked the dynamics of abuse. They do not address the issue of violence against women and children in their otherwise fine book and neither do the recent journal articles reviewed in Saydah's (1990) article, "Research in Review: The Latest on Family Intervention" (p. 12). This oversight may lead to serious problems for survivors who are caught up in a rehabilitationist's desire to provide family intervention services without knowing that the survivor may be risking her life by returning to the family where her injury was inflicted! What is even worse is that the survivor may be unable to advocate for herself in this regard because of her brain injury or her terror or her denial. The Council for Prostitution Alternatives' data base indicates that 83% of the more than 800 survivors have suffered from aggravated assault(s) (Neland, undated). The executive director knows that some of these women are traumatically brain-injured, and when she is asked what can be done to help these women, she replies, "Love them. What else can we do?" (Hunter & Reed, 1990).

A feminist vocational rehabilitation approach would agree but also demand that the new understanding, methods, and interdisciplinary approaches to the treatment of the battered prostitute, housewife, or child with traumatic head injury be integrated with the new understanding of the dynamics of woman battering, rape, and childhood assaults, both physical and sexual.

...if the shelter system in this country can be said to be a rehabilitation system, it is the only system of rehabilitation for a physically and psychologically injured population without a standard medical and psychological evaluation process.

Shelter budgets do not now include a systematic medical and psychological workup for their clients who are housed in the shelter system, nor for clients who do not come into the shelter but use counseling and support group services. Furthermore, if the shelter system in this country can be said to be a rehabilitation system, it is the only system of rehabilitation for a physically and psychologically injured population without a standard medical and psychological evaluation process. The rehabilitation delivery systems which appear on the right hand (or male side) of Table 1, have medical evaluations , including general physical examinations and other special evaluations depending on the type of injury, which are used to determine standards of care and eligibility. If psychological factors warrant, a general psychological examination will be authorized as well. On the female side of Table 1, no such standardized services exist, and this is because the women served are not perceived as injured and the work programs designed for women are placed inside a social welfare model rather than a vocational rehabilitation model.

So when we consider the fact that one in five women in hospital emergency rooms are there because of woman battering, and that many women do not go to emergency rooms because they don't have the resources to do so, and that prostitution survivors are not counted in any or few of the statistics we now have, it is incredible to think we have no systematic care for these injured populations. There are no memoranda issued to nurses and physicians outlining the types and numbers of injuries, suggested treatments, number of staff needed, medical supplies and facilities required for abuse survivors. Such memoranda were issued in February 1991 to medical personnel in Veterans Administration Hospitals in the United States in preparation for the ground war in the Persian Gulf (U.S. Army Nurse, personal communication, February 16, 1991). Where is the mobilization of services for the injured populations of abuse survivors?

You reported pain, pain, and pain. Ongoing pain. In the buttocks, the lower back. Cramps, vomiting, headaches.

—from Miranda's Story

miranda's story*

Miranda, I hardly knew you. You came in and out of my life, my workers' compensation caseload, like a comet trailing pain and suddenly vanished. Gone. Into the void of the San Fernando Valley and the bleak isolation of your marriage, leaving me alone with questions and my conflicted ethics. By the time my suspicions had worked their way to the surface of my consciousness, you were gone. Lost behind the attorney your husband had selected for you, and the two of them bound in some unspoken patriarchal conspiracy to prevent women (you and me) from speaking candidly to each other. And the attorney screaming at me on the telephone. And me discovering later that he was a coke addict, but that revelation not making his words any easier. The words beneath his words: "Cunt! Bitch! Do it my way or else! How dare you have any power on my turf? With my client?"

All this time has passed now but I still think of you. How you came to my office so pale and washed out even though you were plump and tall. You felt thin and stretched to me. You did not speak except to murmur when politeness demanded. Your husband spoke for you, answered all the questions about your life. When you went to the work hardening program, you refused to give a health history. He gave it. When you went to the physical tolerance evaluation facility, the staff described you as flippant, meaning sarcastic. I wished I'd seen that, your rebellion. Somewhere, anywhere. You never showed it to me.

Instead you said, "I don't read well." Your husband was watching my face. I tried to control my face (sometimes it gets away from me) because I didn't want to give anything away that could be used against you later. Even my eyebrows didn't rise which is, I guess, why they itch now as I write this. It didn't make sense to me that you were not a good

_____

*As told by the author.

reader. There was nothing in your speech patterns, your educational or vocational history which would indicate otherwise. You worked for the same national company as your husband. Ah! That was it. My first clue. If you worked somewhere else, how could he keep track of you? Then there was the car. One car between you and your rehabilitation would have to be arranged around his work hours. He said he would arrange alternative transportation for himself, but together and nonverbally, you and I knew that it would be easier for us to work around his schedule than to assert your needs in rehabilitation.

I searched your medical records: lumbar strain, laminectomy. Nothing odd for a workers' compensation client. There were no records of bruises, marks, tearing of anus or vaginal openings. I wanted a special fine-toothed comb, one which could sweep up unwritten words, stray observations, the stuff between the lines. You reported pain, pain, and pain. Ongoing pain. In the buttocks, the lower back. Cramps, vomiting, headaches. One report alluded to possible psychological complaints resulting from extended medical treatments and procedures. I wanted to shred the reports into confetti and reassemble the pieces. Maybe I could find something. I needed something. I could feel you passing me by. It all ended at the exit conference at the physical tolerance evaluation site. Your husband was there. We all gathered at one end of a long, gleaming conference table in a room with no windows. You sat next to your husband, and there was color in your face. After all, you had spent 10 days without him. He couldn't call you and/or drift by to see what you were doing or to whom you spoke. You sat next to him and patted his arm as he talked, or rather, shouted at me. He was angry about the results of the reading test. Both the evaluator and I explained about nationally standardized testing procedures, national norms. Miranda, it was the only thing I ever gave you. You're a good reader, an excellent reader. Your scores were far above the national average and even past the test's limits.

The evaluator and I explained to you and your husband how important it was for you to make decisions about your own rehabilitation, not your *husband, but you just kept on smiling, nodding, and patting your husband's arm.*

And then you were gone. I was fired the next day by the attorney. I had gotten close, too close. You might have gone to work somewhere else. You might have spoken to me. I always wanted to ask you, "What is it? What is it he does to you? Is it rape? When did it start? Before your back surgery? Afterward? Before and after and during recovery? Your back? Did it happen at work? Or did he do it to you?"

five

---

the abuse of injured
and disabled women

*Miller boasts, perhaps one should say, confesses, that
the "best fuck" he ever had was with a creature nearly
devoid of sense, the "simpleton" who lived upstairs.
"Everything was anonymous and unform-
ulated....Above the belt, as I say, she was batty. Yes,
absolutely cuckoo, though still aboard and afloat.
Perhaps that was what made her cunt so marvelously
impersonal. It was one cunt out of a million....Meeting
her in the daytime, watching her slowly going daft, it
was like trapping a weasel when night came on."
(Millett quoting from Henry Miller, 1970, p. 394).*

---

*I was not born differently abled, neither were the
thousands of women who have been permanently
disfigured, scarred or maimed through battering.* (Hall,
1990, p. 5)

Acknowledging the vulnerability I would deny....
(Donovan, 1987, pp. 31-32).

I'm a member of three minorities: I'm a woman, Asian and disabled. Which do I identify with most strongly? It's like a triangle. It depends on the circumstances which point of the triangle is on top. (Saxton & Howe, quoting Barbara Chin, 1987, p. 10)

Disabled, handicapped, differently-abled, physically or mentally different, physically challenged, women with disabilities—this is more than a mere discourse in semantics and a matter of personal preference. Disabled women is the term which most accurately characterizes our position in American society. (Connors, 1985, p. 92)

At the 1990 *Take Back The Night March Speakout* in Denver, a woman approached the podium. She held a packet of paper, like a small book or pamphlet. As she read, she released the pages one by one as her fingertips raced across the braille, and the pages fell away into a long accordion pleat of white. Her exact words have melted away into all the other stories I heard that night, but her passion has not. It beats against my consciousness like a persistent knock at the door, "I'm here! I'm here! Disabled women get raped, too. Is there anybody home?"

An excellent question. The needs of disabled women have barely been perceived by the rape or the battered women's movements. Disabled women are now demanding access to shelters and to rape and battering recovery services (Grothaus, 1985). The Americans with Disabilities Act may force changes on shelters and agencies offering services to abused women and children. These changes will include installation of ramps and access to kitchens, bathrooms, bedrooms, and meeting facilities. Telephone services for the hearing-impaired will be required (Lamoreauz, 1990). How this is to be financed promises to be a difficult issue for perpetually struggling battered women's shelters and rape crisis centers.

And yet this is an issue which must be faced. If it is not, Baldwin (1990) will have yet another example of the "trickle-down theory of feminism." Baldwin's comments are directed to feminism's paralysis on the prostitution issue and how that paralysis allows us to sacrifice a class of women as expendable, but her comments could include disabled women as well. If this seems harsh or irrelevant, consider the data from the Council for Prostitution Alternatives which indicate that the prostitution survivor population appears to contain large numbers of women with disabilities (Neland, undated): Fetal Alcohol Syndrome (FAS) and Fetal Alcohol Effect (FAE)-15%; Multiple Personality Disorder (MPD)-10 to 15%; Traumatic Head Injury-10%; Incest Trauma- 65%; Child Battering Trauma-69%; Substance Abuse-85%; Rape Trauma-80%; Adult Battering Trauma-95%; Ritual Abuse Trauma-8%; Suicide Attempts-57%. All of these categories, both psychological and physical, can be regarded as disabling conditions, and with the exception of the trauma categories, have been regarded as such by the rehabilitation profession for most of its history.

This is not to suggest that all prostitution survivors are disabled women or that all disabled women are prostitutes, but rather to point out once again the value of putting prostitution at the center of the rape paradigm. Henry Miller's crude, woman-hating description of his rape of a mentally retarded and/or mentally ill woman is a good example of the pervasive character of the rape paradigm which spares no one, not even the most vulnerable of women. Miller's ideal woman, who Millett (1970) describes as a "whore"; also turns out to be a disabled woman.

When these connections are made, one is forced to wonder what the actual rape and assault rates are among disabled women. One also wonders how many disabled women are forced into prostitution because of their disabilities. The barriers to reporting rape, assault, and extortion to engage in prostitution are the same for disabled women as for any woman, but there are added difficulties (Grothaus, 1985). They can include: loss of independent living status (meaning, "put that woman in a safe place"); her sense that battering or rape is deserved because she is so needy; a willingness to "make up" for her lack of physical "beauty"; and a loss of the role of wife or loss of her children because of her "unfit" mother status (Grothaus, 1985). The disabled woman may not report rapes and/or assaults because she is mentally incapable or cannot communicate.

Although rehabilitationists are not unaware of abuse among their disabled clients, they tend to make decisions about the client's core issues without finding out which one of the points of the triangle, as Barbara Chin (Saxton & Howe, 1987, p. 10) puts it, happens to be on top. One identity cannot be sacrificed for another.

Henry Miller's crude, woman-hating description of his rape of a mentally retarded and/or mentally ill woman is a good example of the pervasive character of the rape paradigm which spares no one, not even the most vulnerable of women.

Rehabilitationists have a long way to go as the two case summaries presented below will reveal. The cases are drawn from the Private Rehabilitation Suppliers of Georgia Ethics and Standards Committee (1989) in their publication, *Ethical Issues In Private Sector Rehabilitation.*

The first case is a good example of what Grothaus (1985) writes: "Disabled women, no matter the subject being explored, are an invisible population" (pp. 124-130).

Case 1

A Private Rehabilitation Practitioner (PRP) was assigned to work with a client who was raped by a customer of the store where she was employed. The client was diagnosed as having schizophrenia in addition to experiencing post-traumatic stress disorder. The client was admitted to an expensive, private psychiatric hospital for treatment. The facility psychiatrist, a close friend of the PRP, was designated as the client's primary physician.

After a two-month hospitalization, the psychiatrist felt that the client was ready for discharge from the facility and able to participate in vocational rehabilitation. The PRP and psychiatrist recommended retraining even though the previous employer was willing to create or modify a position for the client. When the claims representative would not agree to pay for the client's retraining based on the availability of suitable jobs with the previous employer, the psychiatrist then stated the client was not stable enough to be discharged from the facility. Three months later, the client was still hospitalized for treatment.

Alternatives

1. The claims representative could arrange for an independent psychiatric evaluation.

2. The claims representative could confront the PRP and the psychiatrist with his/her feeling that a conflict of interest appears to exist.

3. The claims representative could change PRPs.

4. The claims representative could file an ethics complaint of conflict of interest against the PRP based on documentation that the PRP and psychiatrist were in collusion.

5. Other (p. 63).

Huh? Where to begin? What happened to the client in this story? Remember her? The raped woman with a diagnosis of schizophrenia and post- traumatic stress disorder? The ethical issue presented here by the authors revolves around the relationships among the claims representative, the PRP, and the psychiatrist, and boils down to who gets what money. The claims representative is suddenly the person with the problem. Is it just accidental that the only person in this story with a specified gender is the rape victim? Is this to suggest that the genders of the PRP, the psychiatrist, or the claims examiner have no bearing on the case at all because these are "professionals" and are, therefore, "objective"?

If this case summary was written to explore conflict of interest issues, why choose a rape story? This is the only rape story in the 32 case summaries presented. Was the rape story presented because rape is "sexy" and makes the case more "exciting"?

Finkelhor and colleagues (1983) have written that "abuse tends to gravitate toward the relationships of the greatest power differential" (p. 18). The very presentation of this case is abusive to both disabled and raped women since it renders them invisible and as objects to be used to discuss other issues, other ideas.

If we are to take this case as "real," then the PRP, the claims examiner, and the psychiatrist must be categorized as abusers of a raped and disabled woman. Her injury and her disability are being used to create wealth for the psychiatrist and the PRP. The claims examiner and the employer appear to be in collusion over settling this workers' compensation claim at the least cost to them without regard for the client's needs or wishes.

Her wishes or needs are unknown. Does the client feel ready to return to work? Rape survivors with PTSD may experience flashbacks when they return to the place where the rape took place. This client may never wish to return to her former employment setting. Some survivors lose entire professions or occupations because of Rape Trauma Syndrome (see *Sandra's Story* or *Harriet's Story*). Others are unable to return to buildings or settings which remind them of the rape experience (see Table 2). The empowerment of this client, which should be the most important issue in this case, seems to be least important.

The following case appears to have a visible client, a disabled woman who is present, but as we shall see, she also vanishes from the story of her own life.

Case 2

A 20-year-old represented, married female client without children was referred to a PRP for medical care coordination. The client had not worked for eight months. The client's workers' compensation claim had been controverted; however, after litigation, the insurance carrier had been ordered by the state regulatory agency to accept the claim. The carrier had voluntarily made the referral to the PRP as the client had a limp in one leg with acute pain, the cause of which was undiagnosed.

At the time of the PRP's initial visit with the client and her unemployed 22-year-old husband, it was learned that the client had an appointment for an independent medical evaluation with the head of the department of orthopedic surgery at a local medical school.

During this visit, the client appeared pale, had several areas of discolored skin and was guarded in all her body movements. Based upon observations during the course of the next few contacts with client, the PRP began to suspect the client was being physically abused. As a result, the PRP confronted the client and her husband with these suspicions. They both freely admitted that the husband had an alcohol and drug problem, and at times became abusive. In fact, the client stated that in the past, she had shopped physicians to acquire prescriptions for "pain killers" ostensibly for herself, which had been billed to the carrier, but were for her husband. Following this confrontation, the PRP discussed in detail the community services available to the client for abused women and offered to assist the client in obtaining these services if she so desired. With the client's permission, the PRP informed the client's attorney and the carrier's attorney of the client's situation. A diagnosis of vascular necrosis was made by the independent medical examiner orthopedic surgeon with a recommendation for a total hip replacement. Following this procedure, the client elected to recuperate from the surgery at her parents' home in order to distance herself from her husband whom she was considering divorcing. However, after several weeks, she returned to live with her husband stating that she could not tolerate living with her parents. Apparently, both of her parents were alcoholics and she was afraid she would be abused by them as she had been as a child. A month later the client said she was afraid to leave her husband because she was now pregnant. The PRP continued to offer to help direct the client to available community services for families with alcohol, drug and abuse problems.

The PRP, with the client's consent, kept the client's attorney, carrier's attorney, and the orthopedic surgeon informed of the family's problems. The client's attorney had stated that he/she was only involved in the workers' compensation claim and had refused to represent the client in any possible divorce proceedings. The orthopedic surgeon stated, due to his affiliation with a medical school, that he could not get involved in an "abuse case." The carrier, through its attorney, stated, "Keep on top of it: Do what needs to be done within the limits of our responsibility and nothing more."

What are the PRP's alternatives?

Alternatives

1.   The PRP could continue to support the client emotionally, recognizing that the client probably would take no action to protect herself.

2.   The PRP could ask the client's parents and siblings to help protect her, recognizing that they were probably aware of the situation and to date had not intervened.

3.   The PRP could inform the police despite knowing that the police in the community in which the client lives would be reluctant to take action.

4.   The PRP could ask that a different PRP be assigned for a second professional opinion.

5.   The PRP could suggest that the case be closed, after determining that further services would not result in improvement of the client's condition or status. This would be based upon the fact that the continued disability is, quite likely, the result of physical abuse rather than the work-related injury or lack of appropriate medical treatment. Prior to closure, the PRP could make every effort to assure that the client and family members are aware of available community resources to assist with their situation.

6.   Other (pp. 46-47).

The PRP confronted the client and her husband with these suspicions: Did the PRP have an armed guard when she/he confronted this couple? Does the gender-neutral PRP have an ethical obligation to his/her own life? What about the life of this battered and disabled woman? To her husband? Battered women are sometimes killed by their battering husbands, and sometimes battered women kill their battering husbands (Browne, 1987). And sometimes, battering husbands kill or injured those who interfere in the relationship between husband and wife. In *Liz's Story*, the battering husband threatened to kill helpful bystanders after he had punched Liz in the face, knocking her out.

The PRP confronted the client and her husband with these suspicions: This is equivalent to getting together a street mugger and his victim and informing them that "this kind of behavior has to stop. And, by the way, would you please both go to counseling?"

The PRP confronted the client and her husband with these suspicions: The client now loses all the identities she possesses: disabled woman, battered woman, and worker. She is crushed into that entity we call "family." Her social role as wife and pregnant woman obscures her role as a worker with an independent work identity, and her battering history now eliminates her identity as an injured worker, a disabled woman.

The client now loses all the identities she possesses: disabled woman, battered woman, and worker.

They both freely admitted that the husband had an alcohol and drug problem, and at times became abusive. In fact, the client stated that in the past, she had shopped physicians to acquire prescriptions for "pain killers" ostensibly for herself, which had been billed to the carrier, but were for her husband: These statements can be placed within the rape paradigm. That is, she chooses to be battered. ("Rape" being used here as a term of art referring to all assaults by men on women.) We can infer this because she was one of the people in the "they" who "freely admitted" that her husband abused her and used drugs. Why, she even cheated the insurance company to get drugs for the guy! So, she must love him, wants to stay with him, and chooses to be with him. Right? So this battering, this drug abuse, and this cheating on her husband's part, must be her fault. Right? The husband's criminal and felonious behavior is unacknowledged. No alternative is listed filing criminal charges against the husband for defrauding the insurance company out of money for prescription drugs.

I suggest that disabled women have much to teach the rape and battered women's movements and the rehabilitation profession.

One can almost hear the cliches (*She must like it. Otherwise, why does she stay? Why doesn't she just walk out the door? Just leave?*) rolling around in the head of the poor, well-intentioned PRP who has done everything she/he could, even fulfilling the ethical obligation to refer the family to available community resources as per the professional standards of his/her professional organization (see Appendix 4). And even though the case data indicate that the client did leave her husband and wanted a divorce, the authors (Private Rehabilitation Suppliers, 1989) are so caught up in the choice model of battering, they ignore their own facts and blame the victim one more time by writing, "...the client would take no action to protect herself (pp. 46-47)." The all-encompassing nature of the choice model of battering in this case summary is also demonstrated by the appalling alternative number five which suggests the abandonment of this pregnant, battered, and disabled woman because "further services would not result in improvement of the client's condition or status (pp. 46-47)."

I selected "other" as my alternative solution to this case. It is possible to provide services to disabled and battered women inside the vocational rehabilitation counseling process. Chapter Eleven provides a feminist vocational rehabilitation model which outlines an approach to such cases by rehabilitationists.

In my analysis of these case summaries, I do not mean to denigrate the very real problems faced by rehabilitationists in offering services to women who are disabled and abused. In fact, *Miranda's Story* was written to reveal the sometimes devastating and impossible situations confronting both the disabled woman and the rehabilitationist. As I suggested in Chapter One, we need to listen and learn from prostitution survivors. In this chapter, I suggest that disabled women have much to teach the rape and battered women's movements and the rehabilitation profession. In fact, the 1990 Americans With Disabilities Act may offer a unique opportunity for disabled women to emerge as leaders, who can then teach us how to make the appropriate connections between disability and abuse.

Grothaus' (1985) comment, "Disabled women, no matter the subject being explored, are an invisible population (p. 124)," should be emblazoned in the hearts and minds of every person providing rehabilitation services to disabled and injured women. Until this happens, disabled and injured women will continue to vanish from the stories of their own lives along with their pain, their hopes, and their dreams. They are then lost among the world's "disappeared."

After sex I felt cheap, dirty, ugly. I guess rape victims feel that way but the difference is that he was my husband and I trusted him.

—from *Grace's Story*

grace's story*

I'm a white twenty-eight year old and I'm not sure if I'm an abuse survivor at all. I have a bachelor's degree in psychology and I'd like to go to law school. I was thinking about this interview last night and then I had a dream. It was a strange dream. It took place in my office at the bank. My father was a depositor at the bank, in my dream, but not in actuality. He had opened several accounts which totaled a large amount of money. He decided he was going to withdraw all his money from the bank. I was very angry with him about this. I felt he was choosing to not support me or my activities. I was enraged. This rage even woke me up, but the odd thing was that I let my Dad get away with it in the dream because he gave me a choice in two letters. One letter said that he would leave his money in the bank if I did everything he told me to do. The other said he would take everything out if I didn't follow his explicit instructions.

So I ended up being the bad guy because if I didn't follow his direction, my bank would lose money. I was so angry. I don't know if I've ever felt like that before. I think it connects to Gordie. It feels very similar because I set it up so that it was never his fault, always mine. Gordie is my husband. We are separated now but when I look back, I see I would excuse him by saying, "Well, I wasn't a good enough cook. Or I wasn't supportive enough."

A good example would be the day he came home and announced that he had taken a job in Boise, Idaho, and we were moving. I had just started my MBA. So it's like the dream. Follow the instructions exactly or lose the marriage or face the withdrawal of support. We had been married six weeks when this was presented to me, but I had known him for five years before that, and we had been dating for a year before our marriage.

---

*In her own words.

We got married right after I got my B.A. and he knew I had been admitted to the MBA program. He has three years of college. He was working when we married. I had worked at a bookstore but took the summer off between my graduation, marriage, and starting my MBA program in the fall.

I guess the abuse started before the marriage, if you want to call it abuse. You know how young lovers are. You fuck all the time. I didn't realize that there was zero physical contact outside of sexual intercourse. It was a good three months into my marriage before a light bulb went on. I approached him with it. I said, "Wait a minute. There's nothing here except for intercourse. We don't have any cuddling, closeness, or even hand holding."

I guess there was some foreplay or else I would have been too dry, but we were having sex once or twice per day. It was about as exciting as brushing one's teeth. I never had a problem with orgasm or anything like that but I wanted cuddling, love. He would approach me by saying, "You want to bone it up?" Stupid really. I felt like I was whoring for a few kisses.

After this confrontation, our frequency of sex declined sharply. I guess the choking started then, too. We would be sitting next to each other on the couch in front of the television set, which was always on, and all of a sudden he'd be choking me with both hands around my neck. I never turned blue or gagged or anything like that. I would say, "Now stop that! This is not proper in marriage." And he would always say, "But honey, this is a loving thing I do for you."

Well, let's see. It went on for two years probably two to three times per week. I weigh 115 pounds and Gordie weighs around 170 pounds. I was very aware of his larger size and strength. Sex followed choking about 90 percent of the time. He always choked me during the late night news before bedtime. We only had sex in the bedroom, in our bed. He was very particular about that. I felt it was my obligation as a wife to service him.

I never really connected the choking and the sex before. Once he said to me, "If you ever left me, I would hunt you down. I would find you, and I would chop your body into a million pieces and stuff you in the freezer.'' There were other things. He got very angry. He would clench his teeth and breathe really heavy and sweep everything off the table. It was always in the back of my mind though. He feels choking me is acceptable. He has these little fits of rage. One of these days they're going to connect and he really will hunt me down and chop me up.

Do you really think moving to Boise had something to do with all of this? The new job wasn't a step up. The plan was that I would work. I didn't even think about going back to school. Isn't that silly? I had been in the MBA program for six weeks when we moved. Honestly, I hated it but it was only a year program, and I thought I could endure it. I knew it would definitely help me. So, I was relieved when we left. It was an opportunity to quit and save face. It's true, the choking behavior did start in Boise.

It was horrible. I mean, the first month was kind of interesting. It was Christmas time, and he was managing a book store. I could work with him there. Free labor and I knew a lot about books and retailing. I was the perfect little wife. I had to go to the book store because he worked 12 hours per day. He lived there. So if I wanted to see him, I went to the store.

Then I couldn't find a job. I didn't know anyone. I had no contact with my friends. We did visit my family but we did it in one day. Five hours of driving back to the coast, a two hour visit, and back to Boise for another five hours. He was very rude to my family. He was cruel to my sister who has a tendency to babble, to repeat things she doesn't understand. He would put her down in front of everyone. She was a teenager at the time. She was mortified. Yes, he did that to me, too. He would tell me to shut up in front of our friends. I was humiliated, but I made a joke out of it. This went on throughout our marriage.

I didn't get a job for four months. Some days I didn't even get out of bed and get dressed. He was the only one bringing in any money. Finally, I took a job beneath me as a telephone operator in a bank. I took it because I needed the contact with other people. I just decided I was going to be the best telephone operator they ever had, and I was. They promoted me within six weeks, and again and again. I got promoted three or four times in my first six months. I became a real estate loan officer. It was the mid-eighties and real estate was booming. After one and one half years, I had my own department. I was really good.

Then I began to wonder why my life at home was so different from my life at work. I said, "Whoa! Wait a minute. Something is very sick in our relationship. He's not at all happy that I am becoming his equal." I was earning the same amount of money as he was. We were both making around $25,000 per year. A girlfriend of mine pointed this out when I asked Gordie for some money to buy myself some underwear. I was the perfect little wife. I did all of the housework, all of the cooking. I worked 40 hours per week outside the home. I was this dependent weird thing. I waited on his approval. He controlled all the money. I handed my check over to him.

Then I went off to real estate school. I met people who told me I was a good person, a smart person. I began to assert myself at work, and then at home. Another woman at the bank had been in counseling. She recommended it, and so I called them. It was through work, the Employee Assistance Program. My boss was very supportive. They even paid me while I went to counseling. I went about 10 times. The counselor said that he didn't see how Gordie and I could make it unless Gordie came in with me for joint counseling. Gordie was absolutely unwilling. He said, "I don't have a problem. You have the problem." He was horrible to live with on the days I had counseling. He'd pick, pick, pick. Criticize me. The choking stopped after my first counseling session. I said, "I won't tolerate this anymore. Period. I just won't tolerate it." Oh, he tried, but I held firm. I think my going for counseling really scared him and it did stop. I think our marriage died at that point. I insisted on separate checking accounts. I insisted on paying my own bills. We became roommates. We never stayed home alone together. We went out. We were busy, busy, busy. We had season tickets to the theater, soccer, basketball. It was Grace and Gordie—gone, gone, gone.

Then he got a new job in Seattle. My friends told me to leave him. It was the perfect time. He didn't need me anymore, but I wanted to save him. I wanted to make the marriage work. I guess I expected a miracle. I talked to him about separation, and he just fell apart. I thought, "He needs me! I have a responsibility." So I went with him. After one month in Seattle, I went into a panic. It's happening again. Just like Boise. So I took the first job I interviewed for. I'm still there. It was a $10,000 per year pay cut.

After that I had a weekly talk with him, at him. The last time I was just pouring my heart out about how unhappy I was. He would respond with, "Oh honey, you're just tired. You have PMS." The last time, he went over and picked up the newspaper and started reading in the middle of my sobbing. Then I knew. No matter what I said or did, he didn't care. He was never going to make any kind of change because he didn't feel change was necessary. Eventually, we separated. He didn't leave me alone until he found out I was seeing someone else. So, we're working on the divorce.

I guess I need more counseling, but it's so scary. I just dreaded going before. Just dreaded it. It's so hard, making decisions, being honest with yourself. It's so much easier for me to hide behind this whole facade. Everything healthy and cutesy. It's very difficult to make the choice, to dig in, and get down to the nitty gritty. I mean when I talk about it, and I realize I'm not exaggerating, it's pretty bad. I'll say, "Well, I wasn't beaten up physically, but I was emotionally." But the choking did hurt me, and I felt shame about it. Humiliation and embarrassment. After sex I felt cheap, dirty, ugly. I guess rape victims feel that way but the difference is that he was my husband and I trusted him.

six

---

the rehabilitationist as expert witness

When I, as a rehabilitation professional, enter the courtroom, all thoughts of client advocacy are removed from my mind. I have one sole purpose in that courtroom, regardless of whether I have been retained by a plaintiff's attorney, a defense attorney, or an insurance company. My responsibility is to the judicial system and to present fair, professional, and unbiased testimony to the judge and/or jury so that they have adequate data on which to base their conclusions. Anything less than a truly unbiased perspective damages the system and may prove harmful to both the client and the professional. (Deutsch, 1985, p. 4)

Disrespect for female witnesses and expert witnesses and their accomplishments, such as the failure to accord them their appropriate titles, is commonly practiced. One woman attorney believed that she received lower damages in a case involving claims of emotional distress because her client, her client's treating physicians, and her experts were women. She believes that the totality of the effect on the jury was to make her case less believable. (Judicial Council Advisory Committee On Gender Bias In The Courts, 1990, p. 59)

But it isn't really correct to call you Doctor, is it-un-uh, is it Miss, or Ms....? (Ms. will be pronounced "Mizzz," with teeth showing through the prosecutor's extra wide smile.) (Walker, 1989, p. 313)

To raise questions about an expert witness' objectivity, may defense counsel ask the witness whether the expert was a victim of child abuse, rape, or domestic violence? (Myers, 1991, p. 9)

Creating hypotheticals or making theories about the work lives of abuse survivors is perhaps the most important task of the rehabilitationist who provides litigation consultation and expert witness testimony in cases involving abuse issues. And if the vocational expert is the ultimate determiner of work disability, not the physician nor the psychologist, then it is the responsibility of the vocational expert to be as well-informed as possible not only in vocational issues but also in the dynamics of abuse (Williams, 1990).

At the present time, role models for the provision of expert witness testimony regarding incest, rape, and battering come from the criminal justice system, and rarely from the civil litigation process. The rehabilitationist's work is most commonly found in the civil litigation arena (Graham, 1990). Rehabilitationists may be found testifying in Social Security administrative hearings; before workers' compensation administrative judges or referees; in personal injury lawsuits involving automobile accidents, medical malpractice, third party or wrongful death cases; in employment law cases including wrongful termination and sex discrimination (sexual harassment) cases; and in dissolution of marriage cases.

The nationwide implementation of no-fault divorce has resulted in a need for experts to determine the vocational potential of spouses seeking spousal support. In some states, qualifications for experts providing such testimony have been codified into the law books (California Civil Code 4801 (a)-(f), 1992, Nevada Revised Statute 125.150 (8), 1991).

Creating hypotheticals or making theories about the work lives of abuse survivors is perhaps the most important task of the rehabilitationist who provides litigation consultation and expert witness testimony in cases involving abuse issues.

I predict the use of vocational experts in the 1990s by abuse survivors in civil suits ranging from domestic tort law cases to suits brought under a congressional civil rights bill for victims of hate crimes. My prediction is based on the emergence of successful civil suits brought by survivors in the 1980s (Institute for the Study of Sexual Assault, 1983-1987).

Karp and Karp (1989, p. x) write, "Violence, abuse, and disease within the family thus are serving as the bases for an emerging body of tort law, the exact parameters of which have yet to be determined." This emerging body of tort law is described as domestic tort law, and it promises to lead to "a proliferation of tort claims arising out of divorce cases and family disputes" (Karp & Karp, 1989, p. xi). The connections between no-fault divorce and domestic tort law have important ramifications for the preparation of testimony by vocational experts. These ramifications will be explored in Chapter Seven.

Civil suits arising out of sexual assaults, both childhood sexual assault and rapes of adult women, are phenomena of the 1980s (Institute for the Study of Sexual Assault, 1983-1987). Although expert witness testimony by vocational experts was rarely used in these cases, it is my opinion that such decisions (not to use vocational experts) are based on a failure to perceive the victim's work identity, and therefore her possible lost earning capacity which may have arisen out of vocational impairment caused by the assault. As vocational experts become more visible in the legal arena, it is reasonable to expect the use of vocational experts in civil suits brought on the behalf of sexual assault survivors.

If Dworkin and MacKinnon (1988) succeed in their attempts to establish pornography as sex discrimination, then vocational experts may find themselves asked to provide expert witness testimony as to the lost earning capacities of women and children used in pornography.

The Council for Prostitution Alternatives (CPA) is now lobbying the sponsors of the Violence Against Women Act (Senate Bill 2754 and House Bill 5468) to include prostitution survivors in the provisions of the bill (S. K. Hunter, personal communication, March 28, 1991). Sponsored by Senator Joe Biden (D-Delaware) and Representative Barbara Boxer (D-California), the bill contains a civil rights component which would define gender-motivated crime as "hate" crimes which deprive victims of their civil rights. Victims of such crimes would be allowed to bring civil suits against perpetrators ("Major Federal Legislation" 1991). If the CPA succeeds in their lobbying efforts and if this bill passes in the 1990s, then the ground-breaking work done by Dworkin and MacKinnon (1988) for prostitutes used in pornography could be expanded outside of the pornography issue. An increase in the number of civil sexual assault suits filed can also be predicted.

Chapter Ten is a feminist vocational expert's analysis of the Francine Hughes case, which became famous in a book and a television movie with the same name, *The Burning Bed.* This case provides an opportunity to explore wrongful death issues and loss of pleasure in life or hedonic damage concepts. Hedonic damages are usually given in wrongful death cases. The loss of the enjoyment of life and the pleasures of life have been recognized as far back as the Babylonian Code of Hammurabi. In the United States, the legal theory is that life has a measurable monetary value greater than the traditional awards made for financial damages (Smith, 1988). The concept of hedonic damages is also used to help assess damages for pain and suffering or shortened life expectancy (Smith, 1988). Economists are now being used as experts to assist juries in determining how to analyze the value of hedonic damages. The use of vocational experts in offering testimony as to the hedonic damages of the loss of work identity or the loss of a profession or occupation due to abuse has not been attempted. However, Magrowski's 1990 study of 2,000 randomly selected hedonic awards brings vocational expert witness testimony into the hedonic area in a concrete way, and may provide a basis for the concepts of hedonics in abuse cases resulting in vocational impairment and loss. The whole concept of hedonic damages is still controversial and in 1988, only a few states allowed for compensation for the loss of life and the loss of the pleasure of living (Smith, 1988). The notion of hedonic damage awards for the loss of work identity and occupations or professions as the result of abuse promises to be controversial as well.

The following description of the areas of expertise needed by a vocational expert is adapted from Graham's (1990) seminar materials (#1-12) as follows:

The vocational expert is a professional who possesses the following areas of expertise related to assessment, employability and wage loss analysis, labor market information, and rehabilitation planning of vocational issues of the injured individual:

1. Knowledge of the field of vocational rehabilitation including federal and state laws and regulations of pertinent programs;

2. Knowledge of vocational, educational, and psychological assessment procedures, including tests, work samples, situational evaluations used in the assessment of vocational potential;

3. Knowledge of and ability to utilize standard references covering issues of workforce, labor markets, occupations, wage data resources;

4. Knowledge of and ability to determine transferability of skills and to utilize this analysis process in determining loss of vocational functioning as the result of injury or trauma;

5. Knowledge of and ability to analyze jobs for both previous and possible future employment as they exist in the local economy;

6. Ability to determine the potential for probable future employment of the injured worker's transferable skills and capacity to work and the ability to calculate a loss of access to particular jobs that exist in a local economy as the result of the injury's disabling effects;

7. Knowledge of wage earnings data for jobs that exist in the economy. Ability to calculate a wage loss based upon the injured worker's loss of access to employment in that economy. The ability to calculate the loss of power to earn money as a result of injury and the ability to provide employment and earning data for the purpose of calculating the loss of future earnings that is fair and defensible;

8. Knowledge of and ability with procedures, processes, and resources for rehabilitation planning and/or training relative to the physical and/or psychological needs of the injured worker including clinical interviewing skills, functional assessment procedures, capacity evaluation, planning for services such as medical treatment, education, vocational training, job analysis workups and job placement;

9. Ability to present vocational data in depositions and judicial hearings;

10. Ability to serve as a consultant to other professionals involved in the total rehabilitation process of the injured worker;

11. Ability to assist attorneys in the development of case presentation strategy including the development of depositional and trial questions for opposing experts.

12. Ability to present written reports of findings and opinions.

For vocational experts providing services to abuse survivors, I would add:

13. Knowledge of rape shield law provisions and the ability to discuss the implications of obtaining history of abuse experience(s) prior to the assault in question with plaintiff's attorney (e.g., In sexual harassment cases, plaintiff's attorney may not wish a childhood sexual history to be discoverable by the defense.).

14. Knowledge of and ability to explain PTSD and its subcategories, Rape Trauma Syndrome and Battered Woman Syndrome;

15. Knowledge of and ability to use such assessment instruments as the PTSD-I (Watson, Juba, Manifold, Kucala, & Anderson, 1991) or The Abuse Assessment Inventory (Yegidis, 1989).

16. Knowledge of the common physical injuries of abuse survivors and their impact upon vocational function;

17. Knowledge of and ability to explain the prostitution as the center of the rape paradigm concept, particularly in cases involving prostitution survivors and women and children used in pornography and/or prostitution;

18. Knowledge of the "vulnerable years" for rape, including marital rape and inducement/extortion into prostitution (13 to 16 years), and the impact of rape on vocational identity formation;

19. Knowledge of and ability to explain work patterns by gender, race, age, marital status, including educational attainment levels, labor market access, and wage differentials;

20. Knowledge of women's unwaged work lives which may include child care, elder care, and housework, and the impact of the injury on both the unwaged and waged aspects of a woman's worklife;

21. Knowledge of the inappropriateness of confusing or subsuming a woman's work identity with or under her social role of wife and/or mother;

22. Knowledge of the importance of child care considerations in all vocational planning assessments and efforts for injured workers with children;

23. Knowledge of domestic tort law which creates a framework for a lost earning capacity analysis based on the impact of domestic violence;

24. Knowledge of the hedonic value of professions/occupations above and beyond the value of lost earnings; and

25. Knowledge of how to respond to questions about your own possible abuse history which might disqualify you as a witness because of "bias" (Myers, 1991).

All cases presented in this book fall into the "food-for-thought" category. There are no history, no case law, and no legislative responses which might guide us in the development of hypotheticals. Cases presented, then, are to be regarded as demonstrative in nature and not as finished products.

I have selected *Grace's Story* as the first case subjected to a lost earning capacity analysis because, relatively speaking, this is an easy case to analyze and present. As we shall see in Chapter Seven, Grace would not be able to raise the issue of her marital rape experience in a no-fault divorce process. Therefore, Grace and her attorney would need to turn to domestic tort law to raise the marital rape issue. The data presented below are based on an assumption that the attorney has requested information to lay a foundation for damages in a domestic tort suit.

It is the task of the attorney to determine how vocational expert analyses will be used in filing suits. Therefore, I am not trying to practice law. Any discussions of where and how suits might be filed for abuse survivors are merely suggestive and do not imply acceptance by any judicial system. However, as we shall see in the subsequent chapters, preparation of lost earning capacity analyses and other vocational analyses can be used in a variety of legal settings which may or may not involve the filing of a lawsuit. Sometimes the analysis is important because it empowers the survivor. In other words, vocational analyses can have a value above and beyond a day in court or financial damage awards.

The first task is to identify Grace as a worker. In her story she states: *I was the perfect little wife. I did all of the housework, all of the cooking.* Therefore, Grace was a homemaker, an unwaged worker. Grace's waged work identity includes her work at a bookstore during her undergraduate years at college. Her considerable skills and knowledge base in the retailing of books are later used by Grace's husband when he becomes the manager of a bookstore. She has a bachelor's degree in psychology, and she had started an MBA program which was interrupted by her husband's abrupt decision to move to Boise, Idaho. In Boise, Grace gets a job at a bank as a telephone operator and she is quickly promoted to real estate loan officer. Before her husband's second abrupt move to Seattle, she was making $25,000 per year, which was equivalent to her husband's income. Upon her relocation to Seattle, Grace takes the first job she finds because she is afraid of going through the trauma she endured when she relocated to Boise. This job pays $10,000 per year less than the job she left in Boise. The marriage ends.

> *The sudden relocations precipitated by Gordie, Grace's husband, are included within the marital rape/battering dynamic because Grace's wishes in the relocations were never considered.*

The sudden relocations precipitated by Gordie, Grace's husband, are included within the marital rape/battering dynamic because Grace's wishes in the relocations were never considered. Also, the second relocation has the element of two years of marital rape/battering preceding it. It should also be noted that relocation, by itself, is damaging to a career, and could possibly be considered as a loss in the financial settlement of a divorce. Finally, the sudden relocation of wives and families by battering husbands is not an unusual part of the battering dynamic (Bateson, 1991; McNulty, 1980).

Grace was born on May 1, 1962, and she is white. Her worklife expectancy is based on the census and is statistically found to be 24 years in duration from the time of her injury date which is set at September 1, 1986 (Fredlund, 1986-1989). (This is the date Grace would have obtained her first job as an MBA if she had not married Gordie.) Statistical data do not account for individual differences, so Grace may have a worklife expectancy longer than 24 years. But since my approach is to use the most conservative figures in making calculations for damages, the worklife expectancy for Grace will remain at 24 years.

Hypothetical #1: What is the value of the household services provided by Grace from the date of the marriage (5/1/85) to the date of separation (1/1/89)?

Since the inclusion of the value of housework in this analysis **at all** is so unusual, I will take a conservative approach. Even though Grace asserts that she did all the housework throughout the marriage, I will use data which indicate that Grace, as an employed woman, contributed approximately 22 hours per week while Gordie, as an employed man, contributed approximately 11 hours per week (Field, 1989).

The next difficulty is determining how to put a value on housework. "The estimation of household services may not be as easy as simply relating household activities to corresponding jobs in the community and then assuming the community wage rates. It is possible, for instance, for a homemaker to wash and dry clothes while at the same time drive two boys to soccer practice. In terms of wage rates, the value of homemaker production may not equate with marketplace production (Field 1989)." For purposes of this analysis, we will assume that Grace's duties could have been taken over by a housekeeper/cook who came in 7 days per week for two hours at $7.00 per hour for a total of 24 hours. Gordie's duties could have been taken over by a handyman who came in on the weekends for $7.00 per hour for a total of 11 hours (Field, 1989, Leonoesio, 1989). If we assume that the length of the marriage (or time lived together while performing household services) was 182 weeks, then Grace contributed **$30,576** of household services to the marriage, while Gordie contributed **$14,014**.

If there were a way to slap a warning label over these data, I would do it. The label I would like to give you should read: WARNING! THIS MAY BE DANGEROUS TO YOUR ECONOMIC HEALTH. History suggests that the struggle between dominant and alternative paradigms is never simple or short-term. Changing women's economic condition is a centuries-old struggle, and recent history indicates that every effort women make toward economic parity will be used against them by the adherents of the dominant (patriarchal) paradigm.

Warning! This may be dangerous to your economic health.

The best example is the implementation of no-fault divorce which took advantage of women moving into the waged labor market in increasing numbers by creating a presumption that women would go to work in the waged labor market after the marriage ended regardless of the circumstances (Sherman, 1990). This has resulted in economic disaster for women and their dependent children. Therefore, placing an economic valuation on the household and family care services provided by women is fraught with peril. Possible disaster scenarios include comparison of the wife's value as maid, child care worker, and cook to the husband's earning capacity in his waged work as a tool and die maker, engineer, or doctor; demand that the wife use her transferable skills as a maid, cook, and child care worker in the waged labor market regardless of the damage to her vocational development because of the marriage; inappropriate manipulations of the settlement of community property, child, and spousal support payments by using the value of the wife's household and child care services.

However (as we shall see in Chapter Seven), not to value the wife's household and family services is a source of justifiable anger on the part of divorced women. Therefore, household services will be acknowledged in all appropriate cases presented in this book. The dollar values placed on these services are not to be taken as the value of the woman providing the services. That is, marriage is not just about having a maid or a child care worker. It is assumed that quality of life issues are paramount in marriage, and those tasks which the partners perform for each other and their children have a value beyond the monetary.

...marriage is not just about having a maid or a child care worker.

Hypothetical #2: If Grace had been able to complete her MBA, what would her earnings have been from the time of her first job after graduation (9/1/86) to the end of the marriage (5/1/90)? It is assumed that Grace paid for her own MBA through student loans and working part-time at the bookstore 20 hours per week at $5.50 per hour until she got a job after graduation on 9/1/86. Grace's new job had a starting salary of $35,000 per year with benefits equaling 15% of her salary. Grace would have earned approximately $159,007 with her MBA credentials, but instead she averaged a yearly salary of $18,688 (total of $74,752) including a 15% benefit level over this four-year period (U.S. Department of Labor, Bureau of Labor Statistics, 1990-1991; National Association of Business Economists, 1988). She has a loss of **$84,255**.

Hypothetical #3: If Grace had stayed in Boise, what would her earnings have been from the time of the move to Seattle (9/1/89) to the end of her marriage (5/1/90)? The assumption is that Grace continues in her job as a real estate loan officer at the bank making $25,000 per year with benefits at 15% or $28,750. Grace has earnings and benefits of $2,396 monthly. Grace took a secretarial job at $15,000 per year with 15% benefits giving her a monthly total of $1,438. In the move to Seattle, Grace lost **$9,102**.

Hypothetical #4: If Grace continues as a secretary at $15,000 per year with a 15% benefit level throughout her worklife expectancy of 24 years without completing her MBA, what are her losses? (This is not an unlikely scenario since Grace has not yet resumed working on any professional track and she has not attempted to return to graduate school for professional training. Her window of opportunity for a professional career may now be shut because of the abuse.) If Grace had completed her MBA and worked in her profession over her 24-year worklife expectancy, she would have earned approximately $911,840 (U.S. Department of Labor, Bureau of Labor Statistics, 1990-1991; National Association of Business Economists, 1988). As a secretary she will earn approximately $390,788. Her loss will range between $421,763 to $347,314 depending upon the discount rate (Field & Field, 1990).

Noneconomic or hedonic awards in cases involving vocational issues range from **$27,095** to **$209,917** (Magrowski, 1991). Such damages might be appropriate to consider in Grace's domestic tort case.

The most cost-effective response to all of these figures, by Gordie, would probably be an offer to pay for Grace's graduate education so that she could restore her lost earning capacity. Counseling expenses, spousal support, and vocational rehabilitation planning expenses should be included in any such arrangements.

He threatened my friends, my friend's husbands, ``If you help her get this divorce, I'll kill you.''
And people were afraid.

—from *Liz's Story*

liz's story*

I'm one of those nice Jewish girls who was supposed to marry a doctor or at least a successful man. I'm 47 years old now and I was raised in New York City. I have a bachelor's degree in nursing and I've been licensed in New York and Utah. I've worked as a nursing assistant in states where I didn't have a license. I've been trained as a volunteer on a crisis line for a battered women's shelter and I also work there as a relief worker in the shelter.

My mother was a housewife and still is. She worked periodically as a hairdresser, an antique dealer, an interior decorator. My father was a union man in a large corporation as a printer. I have a sister who lives on the West Coast. My sister is in total denial about our background. She gets very defensive and angry when I choose to talk to her—which I do—because my sister remembers more of our childhood than I do. I remembered that I was incested by my father and my mother. This has really shaken me up, about my mother, because everyone else talks about fathers and uncles. It's shaken me up about my sexuality and everything else.

I don't remember my childhood except for the incest. When I was 10 I had developed pubic hair and I was in the bathtub and my father was there washing my hair. He was on his knees in the bathroom. He touched my pubic hair and said, "Oh, I see you have pubic hair." He touched my vagina and asked, "Does that feel good?" It's all I remember. I've had flashbacks during sex of being penetrated while I was on my stomach. I don't like anyone touching my back. I remember a penis in my mouth.

My parents took me to the doctor for something called "nervous paralysis." It's just the way I react to stress. My mouth shuts down and I can't move it.

---

* In her own words.

*I remember knowing that I wanted to be some-
body. I wanted to be a doctor. My grades were
excellent while my sister was failing everything. She
managed to graduate from high school, just barely.
She was having sex at 12 or 13. I know because I
walked in on her once in our bedroom. I wasn't
interested in boys. It was very confusing for me. I
never felt that way. I used to fantasize about touching a girl's breast. I told my mother and she was
horrified.*

*About six months ago I was seduced by a woman
who was very heterosexual in her looks and manner.
I felt very vulnerable, like being a teenager in my
mother's house with her things, her mannerisms. That
night it all played out in front of me when I went to
bed. My mother saying, "Never let a man look at you
down there because it's ugly." I didn't think it was
ugly. My mother had me touch her, put my fingers
inside her. I've written to her about it and my sister
called. She said, "Don't expect to hear from
Mommy."*

*I married my husband when I was still in high
school. It was my mother's idea. Her message was
that she only felt worthwhile when a man would love
her. She would dress up for a man. She always had
men around the house. So I gave up all the power I
might have created for myself or even had, but
didn't recognize. I switched from mother/father/
sister to my husband. My husband was six years older
than me and he told me he knew more than I did. He
was a traveling salesman. My parents and my sister,
and my husband and I all lived in the same apartment building. So I went to college and I had a
miscarriage and my husband and my mother-in-law
took over. So my life was run by everyone but me.*

*I rarely had sex with my husband because I hated
it. I didn't know there were lesbians. I was just never
turned-on. He would show me sex films and I would
always be turned-on by what the man was doing to
the woman because that's what I wanted to do. I used
to masturbate all the time. I knew about orgasms.*

*Then we left New York City because of his work
and moved to different states—Texas, California,
and finally Utah. Somewhere in there I had a nervous*

breakdown. I had another miscarriage, my father died, but my husband wouldn't listen to me or talk to me. I couldn't stop crying. They gave me antidepressants. Then I wanted to file for a divorce. I had an affair with the lawyer I went to. I was doing what my mother would do, but he didn't help me. He told me that it would be very difficult with someone like my husband. He said, "Why don't you just raise the kids?"

So then I tried working as a nurse part-time. My husband was making really big money by now but he didn't like me working at all. I was told that my college degree was to help me raise the children, that he had allowed me to get the degree for that reason only. We only had one car and he would take it with him on trips. This meant I had to beg rides or refuse jobs when I couldn't find one. I had a little wagon I used to get to the grocery store to buy groceries. I worked perhaps less than 100 days altogether in the 20 years of my marriage.

I stopped my awareness at that point. I told myself, "I have everything. I have this nice house. I'm taking care of my children. I have a job I can go to if I want to. I don't HAVE to work so I can stay home." I started running then. I was an avid, competitive runner. I could do that because I could meet people who were doing the same thing and I could still come home and cook and clean and do all that. I began to have affairs with women, but I was still basically "in the closet."

We had been married 20 years when he retired. He started building an experimental airplane inside the house. It took over all our lives, mine and the kids. I thought I was physically fit but actually I was anorexic, the old pattern—my mouth closed, not eating. I weighed 89 pounds. I decided to ask for a divorce on the day he found me in the closet. I had no way to get away from him so I went into the closet in our bedroom. I went into a fetal position. Then he wanted me for something else. Bring him lunch or whatever. I didn't answer him but he knew I was in the house. And so he went looking for me, and he opened up the closet and yelled at me, "What's the matter with you?" I remember my mouth was open and I heard screaming from far away. At the time, I didn't know

*it was me but what I screamed was, "I AM DYING!"
It was my moment. I understood that I was spiritually
dead; I was physically killing myself by not eating. For
what? My mother used to say to me, "Put a smile on
your face and tell him that you love him."*

*I didn't think of it as rape. The day before I went
into the closet he wanted me to bend over and enter
me from behind. I didn't want to but he did it anyway.
I called a women's shelter crisis line and told them I
was sleeping in my bed with a frying pan and my
clothes on and the lights lit. He was sleeping in one of
my son's bedrooms. Finally, I got a restraining order
and he was out of the house. He would break down
the bathroom door and assault me. Sometimes he
would beat me up and then rape me and sometimes
he would rape me and then beat me while he raped
me. I see only out my right eye. He blinded me in the
left one. He broke my nose, too. He told me later that
it was no accident. It was just what he wanted. He
said, "I can have you anytime I want. You're still my
wife. I can do anything I want to you."*

*He wined and dined me to get me to stop the
divorce. He took me to dinner to coerce me into
settling for a separation and not a divorce. I said,
"No." He punched me right there in the restaurant.
I don't know how long I was unconscious but when
I woke up, there were people around and he was
yelling at them to get away. "I'm taking care of this.
It's okay," he said. He threatened my friends, my
friend's husbands, "If you help her get this divorce, I'll
kill you." And people were afraid.*

*But the divorce went through and I used my
settlement money to buy a townhouse and finish
raising my sons. They all lived with me and finished
college. I found a job with a doctor who hired me
because I was a well-known runner and he wanted
my contacts. We started having sex almost immediately. I didn't feel qualified for the job. I felt I was
prostituting myself for the job. He does this with all his
office managers. The sex stopped when I quit the job.
I was just another piece of ass. I became promiscu-
ous with women. I came out of the closet. I started
cleaning houses for work. I started doing therapy.
Actually I've been in therapy my whole life, off and*

on. My recovery started only three years ago, after my first important relationship with a woman who turned out to be a batterer. She beat me up. Turned out she had been a batterer to her sister, but I hadn't known that. I was still in denial. I was into all this codependency talk, but I was still unable to identify battering because she was a lesbian. My new world came crashing down. It happened once. I called the police, and she was put on six-months' probation. Most of us have been abused, so what makes us think it just stops when we live with a woman? I went to six different therapists until I found one I could trust.

I'm proud of myself, but I feel sorry sometimes. I'm 47 years old and it's taken so long and I get scared about the layers that keep surfacing. Vocationally, I'm still doing housecleaning because it's safe. I don't have to trust anyone. It's either clean or it's not, but I have so much potential. How long am I going to keep cleaning houses? There are days—one more toilet bowl. I judge myself, "Is this all you're going to do?" I do work at the shelter. I'm doing incredible, responsible work, and I'm paid $5.25 per hour. If I want to give up my weekends, I can look forward to $8.00 per hour. How come there's no real money for this work?

seven

---

the use of vocational experts in no-fault divorce and domestic tort cases

California's pioneering divorce law reforms spear-headed the transformation of American family law in the 1970s and early 1980s....the California model has been extremely influential; many, although not all, of its key provisions have been widely adopted....All American states except South Dakota now have some form of no-fault divorce. (Weitzman, 1985, p. 41)

In "In Re-marriage of Morrison" (1978) 20 Cal. 3d 437, the Supreme Court explained that it is the policy of this state...that all supported spouses who are able to do so should seek employment... the Legislature expected that courts would issue orders encouraging these spouses to seek employment and to work toward becoming self-supporting. (Sherman, 1990, p. 140)

In more recent years, many exceptions to the doctrine of interspousal immunity have been established , and in some states the doctrine has been completely abrogated....Most jurisdictions now afford legal pro-

cess for a spouse who has suffered physical abuse or injury for his or her marital partner to obtain a remedy for such grievance—either through domestic violence protective orders, criminal prosecution, or civil tort litigation. (Karp & Karp, 1989, p. 28)

The masculinist origins of my profession are never more apparent than when I am called upon to provide services to women in the divorce process. My graduate education in vocational rehabilitation did not include a study of women's work patterns and the continuing education seminars and workshops which meet the requirements for maintenance of professional certification do not provide for study of women's work patterns. And although rehabilitationists are expected to keep up with changes in workers' compensation legislation and case law or federal legislation and case law (e.g., the Americans with Disabilities Act), no such expectation appears to exist regarding changes in divorce laws and their impact on women's work lives.

And yet the implementation of no-fault divorce by most states in the 1970s and 1980s is arguably one of the most important changes in women's work lives in this century.

And yet the implementation of no-fault divorce by most states in the 1970s and 1980s is arguably one of the most important changes in women's work lives in this century. The courts have now mandated "that all supported spouses who are able to do so should seek employment."

Even worse is the rehabilitation profession's lack of focus on the abused woman as a client in need of services, because one of the effects of no-fault divorce is the disappearance of the battered/raped woman in the divorce process. For example, Weitzman's (1985) book on divorce contains no references to wife battering or domestic violence. There are references to rape and to restraining orders, but these references do not lead to any analysis of the impact of the no-fault divorce process on the battered/raped woman going through the process.

This lack of analysis may have also led to Weitzman's (1985) scathing comments about the term *rehabilitative alimony.* She writes:

> The shift from permanent to time-limited alimony awards is also evident throughout the United States. In theory, the duration of these time-limited awards is to be set to allow "the time deemed necessary by the court for the party seeking alimony to gain sufficient education or training to enable the party to find suitable employment." If, however, the California experience is typical, most of these awards are being limited to a few years at the most. (They are often referred to by the insulting term rehabilitative alimony which suggests that the homemaker has not been engaged in productive or socially useful work during marriage.) (pp. 45-46)

Weitzman's comments on this terminology have been influential, and the 1987 *Justice For Women: First Report of the Nevada Supreme Court Task Force on Gender Bias in the Courts* contains the following footnote:

> This form of spousal support is often awarded with the express purpose of rehabilitating an unemployed or relatively unemployable spouse. This term is objected to by many divorced homemakers because of its paternalistic connotation and because of the common use of this term in the criminal justice system. Women justifiably look to transitional support as a due, not as a paternalistic concession. They are not being rehabilitated; they are merely being justly compensated for lost opportunities resulting from the nature of their married lives. (Springer et al., 1987)

It's unfortunate that feminist vocational rehabilitationists have not been available for an explanation of this terminology, because the term *rehabilitative alimony* gives recognition to the damage caused to women by marriage in terms of the vocational impairment which results simply because of not working in the male, waged work world. For example, one category of divorced women is the Displaced Homemaker. The status of these women is roughly equivalent to displaced male workers who lose their jobs when a factory closes. Both displaced homemakers and displaced factory workers are considered to be in need of rehabilitation (i.e., career counseling, vocational evaluation, training/re-training, resumé development, and job leads). Even white male executives who are displaced in corporate mergers are offered outplacement services which have all the features of rehabilitation (Deneen, 1991; Miller, 1989; Trapasso, 1991).

Therefore, to reject the use of the word *rehabilitation* when discussing the vocational concerns of women in the divorce process is to exclude women from an important aspect of work identity development. That is, one way in which this society recognizes an individual as a worker is to compensate that person when the status of worker is lost or impaired. This is done through such systems as unemployment compensation, workers' compensation, and now, rehabilitative alimony.

The rage in both Weitzman's (1985) and the Gender Bias Task Force's (1987) remarks appears to center on the lack of recognition of the value of homemaking and child care activities. The inclusion of an actual dollar valuation of these activities in the divorce process will go a long way in identifying the homemaker as a worker and, perhaps, in establishing a better set of facts for decisions about spousal support and the rehabilitation needs of each woman in the divorce process. (See warning label for use of these facts on in Chapter Six.) This is why the value of household services was included in the economic evaluation of Grace's case in the last chapter. Such an analysis will be carried forward in all appropriate cases in this book.

The smell of "ableism" lingers in this flap over terminology. Disability, injury, vocational impairment–these life difficulties know no boundaries. To be disabled, injured, or vocationally impaired certainly carries social stigma, but do we give in to it when we consider women in the divorce process? Isn't the task, instead, not to denigrate or separate ourselves from the disabled or injured, but to move forward to insure a better quality of life for everyone including the quality of life in waged and unwaged work?

And finally, rejection of rehabilitation terminology in the divorce process means we lose an analysis of the battered/raped woman's experience in the divorce process which would allow us to address her physical and/or psychological injuries arising out of the marriage and the impact of these injuries on both her household services (unwaged, but now valued work) and her efforts in the waged work world.

The smell of ``ableism'' lingers in this flap over terminology.

At the present time, this analysis is missing from the no-fault divorce process and can only be brought forward as a domestic tort. Karp and Karp (1989) state, "The handling of domestic tort cases is not easy. It is not practical to file a civil tort action in every divorce case. Only where there are major damages and a good chance of recovery should the lawyer consider pursuing the tort action through the legal system. Often the threat of a possible suit for personal injuries is more advantageous as a negotiating tool than the lawsuit itself" (p. 73).

California's *Civil Code 4801, Spousal Support Order and Decree of Dissolution-Modification, Revocation, Termination* (1992) notes:

> (a) In any judgment decreeing the dissolution of a marriage or a legal separation of the parties, the court may order a party to pay for the support of the other party any amount, and for any period of time, as the court may deem just and reasonable, based on the standard of living established during the marriage. In making the award, the court shall consider all of the following circumstances of the respective parties:

1. The extent to which the earning capacity of each spouse is sufficient to maintain the standard of living established during the marriage, taking into account all of the following:

(A) The marketable skills of the supported spouse; the job market for those skills; the time and expenses required for the supported spouse to acquire those skills; and the possible need for retraining or education to acquire other, more marketable skills or employment.

(B) The extent to which the supported spouse's present or future earning capacity is impaired by periods of unemployment that were incurred during the marriage to permit the supported spouse to devote time to domestic duties.

2. The extent to which the supported spouse contributed to the attainment of an education, training, a career position, or a license by the other spouse.

3. The ability to pay of the supporting spouse, taking into account the supporting spouse's earning capacity, earned and unearned income, assets, and standard of living.

4. The needs of each party based on the standard of living established during the marriage.

5. The obligations and assets, including the separate property of each.

6. The duration of the marriage.

7. The ability of the supported spouse to engage in gainful employment without interfering with the interests of dependent children in the custody of the spouse.

8. The age and health of the parties.

9. The immediate and specific tax consequences to each party.

10. Any other factors which it deems just and equitable.

The court may also order an examination by a vocational training counselor who is defined as:

A vocational training counselor shall have at least the following qualifications:

1. A master's degree in the behavioral sciences.

2. Be qualified to administer and interpret inventories for assessing career potential.

3. Demonstrated ability in interviewing clients, assessing marketable skills with understanding constraints, physical and mental health, previous education and experience, and time and geographic mobility constraints.

4. Knowledge of education and training programs in the area with costs and time plans for these programs (4801, [a]-[f]).

The following case analysis is an example of how the civil code might be generally applied in a no-fault divorce case.

Liz's divorce (*Liz's Story*) took place in the state of Utah, which has fully abrogated its interspousal tort immunity in *Stoker v. Stoker* 616P2d 590 (Karp & Karp, 1989). This will allow for an analysis of Liz's divorce process not only within a no-fault divorce context but also within the domestic tort framework.

The first task, as always, is to identify Liz as a worker. Liz's primary work experience is as an unwaged homemaker with two children. She provided these services to her family for 25 years. Although Liz did obtain a bachelor's degree in nursing when she was 23 years old, she has used this degree less than 100 days in the waged work world. Her licensure as a registered nurse has now expired and she would need at least one year of college to bring her nursing skills up to date. She would also have to sit for the state examination in order to be licensed or registered in her state. Further, Liz does not want to be a nurse now.

Since the separation (for purposes of this discussion it will be assumed that the divorce process is not yet complete), Liz has worked as an office manager in a doctor's office ($6.50 per hour with no benefits); in independent housecleaning ($7.50 per hour with no benefits); as a relief worker at a battered women's shelter ($5.25 per hour with no benefits). If she works on the weekends, Liz has the potential to make $8.00 hour at the shelter with no benefits. Liz describes herself as confused and frightened about her vocational goals and her future as a worker.

In addition to the vocational impairment brought about by her absence from the waged work world, Liz is a battered/raped woman with a physical disability. The loss of vision in Liz's left eye, as the result of a deliberate beating by her husband, precludes her from jobs requiring depth perception (e.g., working with dangerous machinery, in surgical settings as a nurse) (Deutsch & Sawyer, 1989). Liz's disability means that she has lost her opportunity to work as a nurse even if she wanted to do so. Her lack of depth perception puts her and her patients at risk for HIV infection and many other problems even outside of surgical nursing care environments, since Liz cannot safely give injections or set up intravenous drips. Further, in her community, the labor market for nurses providing administrative services is extremely limited.

For the purpose of analyzing Liz's case, we will assume that she has been diagnosed with PTSD. Walker (1989) categorizes Battered Women Syndrome (BWS) as a subcategory of PTSD. The basic personality traits of a woman with BWS are fear, depression, guilt, passivity, and low self-esteem. These symptoms are then divided into the traumatic effects of victimization (anxiety, physical symptoms), learned helplessness deficits (depression, low self-esteem, problem-solving deficits, apathy), and self-destructive coping mechanisms (guilt, substance abuse, denial) (Campbell, 1990).

Vocational experts wishing to use BWS to support a hypothesis of vocational impairment precluding a woman from full participation in the waged work world will need to be aware of the considerable independent research which supports the presence of BWS in at least some battered women (Campbell, 1990). The vocational expert should be prepared to defend her or his expertise in PTSD, and its subcategory, BWS. Various instruments have been developed to measure PTSD, and the vocational expert should be able to use one or more appropriately (Watson, Juba, Manifold, Kucala, & Anderson, 1991). *The Abuse Risk Inventory For Women* is still in the experimental stages but may be particularly useful for women with low socioeconomic backgrounds (Yegidis, 1989).

The diagnosis of BWS allows us to understand why Liz is unable to move forward vocationally. (I am not precluding the need for a system response to Liz's vocational difficulties, nor am I stating that clinical intervention for Liz is the solution to her problems.)

Liz and I discussed her need to move beyond "one more toilet bowl," and yet provide a service to formerly battered women. We pondered the feasibility of a janitorial business. The financial rewards would not be equal to the standard of living provided by her former husband's income, but might move her beyond the $8.00 per hour barrier where she is now. Additionally, this plan would allow Liz to develop a new set of skills in business. These skills are highly transferable, and Liz could use them in other settings if she should want to move away from her janitorial business. Finally, this plan would allow Liz to feel safe in the familiar while she takes risks with the unfamiliar.

After conducting research into franchised janitorial businesses, I came to the conclusion that Liz would be better off purchasing a carpet cleaning franchise. This is because the profit margin is higher (10% for janitorial and 55% to 65% for carpet cleaning). Carpet cleaning is more flexible than a janitorial business. A janitorial business requires contract arrangements with monthly billings, as well as the challenge of meeting a payroll, since it is difficult to run a janitorial business by oneself. Carpet cleaning, by contrast, is a cash-and-carry business and can be performed by one person for a profit. It would be possible to hire other workers if desired, and the profit margin allows for the purchase of additional equipment with relative ease (Mike Higgins, personal communication, May 1, 1991).

Liz could establish her own carpet cleaning business, and she could hire formerly battered women who wish to enter or re-enter the waged work world. With this business Liz would have both the flexibility and the control she needs now. Liz has already demonstrated her ability to work independently and make a living. These transferable skills would serve Liz well in a carpet cleaning business.

Liz could take community college courses while she develops her business. These courses should include small business management, front-line supervisory training, computerized payroll accounting, marketing and customer relations, and human relations. She should also take courses which would assist her in overcoming self-esteem and problem-solving deficits (e.g., assertiveness training, nutrition, self-defense). Women's studies courses or seminars in women's body image and women in business would be very helpful. She may wish to continue with vocational rehabilitation counseling during the developmental stages of establishing her business as well as participating in psychological counseling as she continues in her recovery.

Liz's birthday is February 7, 1943. Her race is white and by using an injury date of June 1, 1990 (date of the divorce trial or settlement), Liz's worklife expectancy is 9.2 years (Fredlund, 1986-1989).

Hypothetical #1: What is the value of the household services provided by Liz from the date of the marriage-injury date (7/4/61) to the date of the separation (8/28/86)? As a homemaker, Liz worked 55 hours per week, while her husband provided only 5 hours per week of household services (he travelled frequently as part of his work) (Field, 1989). Over the 25 years of Liz's service to her family, she worked a total of 71,500 hours with an average wage at $4.00 per hour totaling $286,000 (Department of Commerce, 1975). Her husband worked a total of 6,500 hours with an average wage of $4.00 per hour for $26,000. Therefore, Liz contributed $260,000 more than her husband in household services.

Hypothetical #2: If Liz were to return to school and upgrade her skills for re-certification as a registered nurse, what would her earnings be if she entered the labor market now? This hypothetical cannot be developed as a vocational rehabilitation plan because Liz has lost her nursing career. The loss of vision in her left eye precludes her from working as a nurse. In a domestic tort case, Liz might be awarded hedonic damages for pain and suffering as a result of this injury as well as hedonic damages for the pain and suffering resulting from her PTSD injury.

Testimony is now being allowed regarding an individual's inability to participate in an occupation for which she has prepared. A study examining how work status influenced noneconomic or hedonic awards indicates that those without occupations received an average award of $27,095.67, while those with occupations received $209,917.40 (Magrowski, 1991).

Hypothetical #3: If Liz had not lost sight in her eye, she could have earned $22,047 per year as a registered nurse by the end of May 1991 (U.S. Department of Labor, Bureau of Labor Statistics, 1991). She would have earned a total of $211,375 by the end of her worklife expectancy. But instead she works as a housekeeper and shelter worker averaging $7.00 per hour or $13,130 per year for a total of $125,882. Her lost earnings over her 9.2 year worklife expectancy range between $77,267 and $70,157 depending upon the discount rate.

What is disallowed in the no-fault divorce process may be allowed in the domestic tort process.

Hypothetical #4: If Liz had vocational rehabilitation counseling leading to the development of a vocational rehabilitation plan, would the vocational rehabilitation effort make economic sense? The plan start date is 6/1/90. The cost of vocational expert witness testimony in depositions and court (both domestic tort and divorce cases), including vocational rehabilitation counseling and plan development, is projected to be between $1,969 to $4,125 based on a range of $50.00 to $75.00 per hour for services (Deutsch & Sawyer, 1989). The projected cost of continued psychotherapy is based on $75.00 per week for 60 months totaling $18,000.

A franchise purchase of a carpet cleaning business is $9,900. Approximately $4,000 is required for a downpayment and the rest can be financed with the franchising company. The purchase covers equipment, six days of training (lodging and travel to the training site are part of the purchase price), instruction manuals, and marketing materials. Liz would also be able to attend conventions and participate in a network of other franchise owners (Mike Higgins, personal communication, May 1, 1991). Liz has already established a house cleaning business, so the van she owns can be used in her carpet cleaning endeavor.

The cost of a two-year community college program, including tuition, registration, books and supplies for two years, starting on 6/1/90 and ending on 6/1/92 is approximately $540.00.

The advantage of this plan is that Liz can put her business into place within a month. The flexibility of the carpet cleaning business will also allow her to continue her housekeeping work while she builds her carpet cleaning work. The business will also allow her the time to attend the local community college. Although it is not possible to easily project earnings for self-employed individuals, it is expected that the carpet cleaning business will allow Liz to break through the $8.00 per hour barrier.

The total cost of vocational rehabilitation, excluding spousal support, is $32,565. Therefore, it appears that rehabilitation does make economic sense, but quality of life sense may be even more important for Liz.

These analyses offer Liz's attorney a powerful tool in both the no-fault divorce process and the domestic tort process. What is disallowed in the no-fault divorce process may be allowed in the domestic tort process. Presently, it is not clear if the psychological and/or physical injuries of abused women can be used in the no-fault divorce process in determining the rehabilitative alimony needs of battered/raped women. For this reason, *vocational experts should prepare no-fault divorce cases as if a domestic tort case will be filed even if the state in which the action takes place has not fully abrogated their interspousal immunity doctrine.* At the very least, such a method will serve to educate formerly battered women, attorneys, and judges as to the vocational impairment which results from abuse.

My job saved my life. If I had lost my job, I don't know what I would have done. It left me with a little piece of self-respect. When I went there, I was somebody.

–from *Harriet's Story*

harriet's story*

I'm white, 29, and the oldest child of three. My sister lives on the East Coast and my brother lives on the West Coast. My parents divorced when I was in college. It was horrible growing up in my family. Everyone is a recovering alcoholic except me. My brother and sister were teenage alcoholics. Everyone is clean and sober now, except my mother. She still abuses. No incest, but lots of verbal abuse by my father. My father also had girlfriends. I walked in on him once in my parent's bedroom. He dated a girl who was in my high school. My mother just pretended it wasn't happening and she buried herself in the women's movement. I was supposed to go the college where my grandfather went. It was a family tradition, but I had to get away. So I went to a small private college as far away from Portland I could get and still get money for school. I got married when I was 21 when I was in my junior year in college. After the marriage I realized I had made a mistake. He wanted to return to his small town in Alberta, Canada and open an accounting firm. I wanted to go to Europe and travel, to live in New York City or Paris. My mother said, "I stuck out my marriage for 27 years. It's not fair that you can just leave."

The catalyst for the breakup was my attraction to one of my professors, a man almost 20 years older than me. It was mutual. I felt in control. No sexual harassment or anything. As soon as I acted upon it, I told my husband and separated from him. I followed this man to New York City. He had obtained a teaching job there. I was so young and naïve. Bob was my second man, the second person I had ever been sexual with. I got a job in a restaurant because I had worked in restaurants before in high school. That first job was a problem because I lowered the skirt on my costume and got in trouble because they wanted it short. Anyway, I became interested in drugs, I'd

---

*In her own words.

been on a high, but I'd never been around cocaine or anything like that. And the women of New York...well they'd been in gangs, and had lots of sex partners, took drugs. We all talked around the waitress station. It was quite an education. I was learning more at the restaurant than I was in my graduate degree program at Columbia.

Then Bob decided we should have an open relationship. Open on his end, but not on mine. Just like my father, but I didn't realize it at the time. So I got my own apartment in New York City. I was 22 years old. I was waitressing and going to graduate school, and I decided there was big world out there and I wanted to see it. So I applied for a part-time job at the Metropolitan Museum of Modern Art, and I got it. It was in the photography department. So I quit graduate school. I had no idea that photography was art. It had never occurred to me. I loved it. I loved my work there. I would stay late at night and go through the collection year by year, starting from the very beginning. I educated myself in the history of photography. I met my batterer there. His work was in the collection. He was a famous photographer. By the time I met him, I had been promoted from receptionist to secretary. I started out part-time but moved into full-time pretty quickly. I continued at the restaurant. I worked at the museum for six years all together, almost the whole time I lived in New York.

Phil stopped by with his portfolio. He came onto me but I said, "No, I'm not interested in getting involved." Somehow, I felt warnings. He kept pursuing me and pursuing me. He was charming, successful, artistically respected. Women just dropped like flies around him, just loved him. But there were these feelings....I noticed when he talked and made jokes, there was a sharp edge to them, cutting. A kind of cruelty, an aloof quality. People really loved him, would be really warm with him, and he would just stand off and be really cool. Not giving.

I held off and held off. Then I was hit by a car on my bicycle. I was seriously injured, requiring hospitalization in intensive care. Nobody from my family came to me even after the doctors called. I was alone. I was afraid. Phil came to visit me. He brought me a little book of photography. I was quite disabled *even after I got out of the hospital. I had broken bones. So he was there and I started dating him.*

Little by little...the control tightening, tightening, and tightening. I was living in my first one-bedroom apartment. I was so proud of it. I thought it was beautiful. It was mine. He came over one day and he wanted to have sex with me, and so I told him how I had just discovered that I had a pre-cancerous growth in my vagina. I asked him to take me to the doctor so I could have the surgery done. I needed someone to take me home. He said, "No way. Forget it." So I had a girlfriend pick me up, and take me home. He went off and slept with another woman. He told me this when he came by after the surgery, and he wanted to have sex with me. I wasn't supposed to have sex. I was in a lot of pain. He insisted upon it. There was a lot of blood. My sheets were just covered with blood. I remember feeling like I didn't have a choice. I didn't have any choice, and if I tried to make a big deal about it, something bad would happen. I would lose him. I remember being afraid.

A week or two later, he came to my apartment and accused me of giving him herpes. "Gosh," I said, "I'll go right down and get checked." He was very angry, screaming and yelling, and accusing me of giving him this thing, that I was contaminated and dirty. I got checked out, and I didn't have herpes. I don't think he ever totally believed it. He had gotten it from the other woman.

A week or two after that, my apartment was robbed. Again, I was afraid. I didn't know what to do. A detective called me a few days later at work saying that there was an emergency. So I rushed home, and the entire street is blocked off, and in my patio lays a young black man with a hole blown in his chest. He was dead. My upstairs neighbor had a .45 magnum and had blown the young man through the window. He landed in my patio. The police wanted to see if I recognized the guy.

I went into trauma. I had never seen anybody dead before. The dead man was also identified as a rapist by rape survivors in the neighborhood. Then the newspapers got hold of it and my name and address were printed all over New York City. Then the telephone calls started coming. Hang ups, all that. The fear all kind of wadded together with my fear about gangs and rapists and what was happening with me and Phil. Phil started carrying one of his guns around. He was into guns. He was going to protect me. He was a big fan of Dashiell Hammett. Then the police talked me into doing a stakeout in lingerie while walking around in my apartment because they were trying to catch other members of the dead boy's gang. The gang members had been spotted in the neighborhood. I kept getting these calls. So, I had to face leaving my first apartment. I was devastated.

In the middle of all of this, Phil says to me, "You ever wanted to be tied up?" I remember being revolted by this but thinking that I had a decision to make: If I say, "No," he's going to leave me. I don't have anybody else. Those creeps are out there and they may try to hurt me. I need someone to protect me, so I'd better say, "Yes." And I'd better just let him do whatever he wants to do. And so all the sexual abuse just blew wide open. I don't want to go into the details. I moved in with him one whole summer.

There was violence about every other day. The physical abuse was only during sex. He never hit me outside of sex. He had guns by the bed. I don't think I had any choice about it at all.

In the meantime, I was continuing to progress at my work. My boss recognized my talent, and I started doing the work of a curator at the museum. But my waitresses job (I've never told anybody this before,)...I had trouble there. The strain was showing up. I was starting to crack. One of the investors in the restaurant started calling me. He was demanding sex. He threatened to get me fired if I didn't sleep with him. This had started before the summer I moved in with Phil. I was able to put him off, juggle things around. I just couldn't do it anymore. So I went to the owner of the restaurant corporation. He wouldn't help so I just gave up. I quit. The museum didn't pay that much. I lost almost $800 per month in income. I'd been working there for two and one half years.

By then Phil was driving me to work and picking me up. I wasn't allowed to use public transportation because of the gang members out there. Just phone calls frightened me. Once, I wanted to go out and ride my bike, but Phil said, "No." I bought into the whole thing. It was full-blown battering by then. Now I was into the whole cycle—physical, emotional, and sexual abuse. It speeded up. Now it was happening two or three times each day. He was happy when I quit the waitress job. He said it was too far away and he didn't like the other waitresses I worked with. He also asked me how I was going to replace the money I had been earning. No offer of help at all.

There were never any marks on my body that others could see. He was very, very careful about that. I told no one. I then became a curator. This had never happened in the history of the museum—a clerical worker becoming a curator. There was a small increase in salary. Phil put me down. He said I was just an assistant, still just a secretary. He said he'd teach me what to do. I had created this new position myself. I created a photographic society. I created a brochure, a program, an organization. I brought in famous photographers from all over the world. It started with a couple of hundred people and now it's thousands. It's still in existence.

My job saved my life. If I had lost my job, I don't know what I would have done. It left me with a little piece of self-respect. When I went there, I was somebody. People liked me, respected me, listened to me. That's how I got through the nights and the weekends.

One woman and her boyfriend became friends of ours. She was a feminist. She took me aside once, and said, "If you ever need anything, I'm here." She gave me her phone number at home. I'd sneak out and have lunch with her. I'd talk to her. She never said anything but I think now she was horrified at what I revealed without me knowing I was doing so.

He made me learn how to use a gun. He made me go to the shooting range. I didn't want to have anything to do with it. I was afraid of guns. He would make me sit for hours and clean the gun. It was getting worse and worse.

I didn't know anything about women's centers or shelters or crisis hot lines. The only thing important in my life was my work, and this was beginning to interfere with that. Ellen wasn't the only feminist I knew. They'd been calling me, the feminist art historians. Asking me to get involved, to write art criticism for them. I knew they were out there. I watched Ellen. She was really strong. One day she told me that her roommate had left, that she had an empty room. I tucked this into the back of my mind. When I got home that night, I told him I was leaving, and he said, "Where will you go? You don't know anybody. There's no place for you." But I knew there was a place for me. I packed my suitcase, called a cab, and left. I just showed up on Ellen's doorstep. She never asked any questions. She just opened the door and showed me my room. The next day she came into the bathroom, and I had my back to her. I know she saw the bruises. From about my armpit level to below my buttocks, one long bruise. I had taken to wearing long skirts by then so they would be covered. I know she saw, but she didn't say anything. Then I told her. Just a little bit though, because I was so ashamed. I was so afraid she was going to make me leave. She was supportive and loving. I couldn't stay there forever so I went to my mother.

The same thing happened. She walked in on me in the bathroom. She saw. She saw my body. She didn't say anything. Some people think it's weird she didn't say anything, but I appreciated it. She didn't need to say it. She was loving and nurturing. She lived in a wonderful house in a small community, such a place of healing. There was a garden, and it was right on the water. I stayed for about three weeks before I returned to the museum. I had taken time off.

I went back to New York City. I got into therapy. I got into feminism and started writing art criticism. I re-entered graduate school. I went to Paris and studied French for my graduate degree. I became a radical lesbian feminist. I couldn't tolerate the museum anymore. I volunteered at a battered women's shelter. I wanted to do something radical. It felt really great, to know that there were other women the same as me. I felt really safe. This was the first place in my life where I didn't have to fight for everything. The staff asked me what I thought, how I felt, and I'd tell them, and they listened! I volunteered for about a year, and then I went on staff. Now I'm the director. I see that I'll be ready to move on in a year or so. I want to make more money, not to live from paycheck to paycheck. But I can't imagine going back to art *history. Never photography because I associate it with the abuse. I tried to go back into my field—but the flashbacks, the memories. I'd like to have a bookstore or a restaurant or a bookstore/café. A political place to be, and then I'll volunteer in the battered women's movement, perhaps on a board. This day-to-day crisis stuff is wearing, but I can't ever completely separate my work from what happened to me.*

eight

the use of vocational experts in civil sexual assault cases

We encourage attorneys who have not undertaken such litigation to recognize that significant recoveries for both adult and child victims of sexual assault are becoming increasingly common. Recovery of money damages by a plaintiff can never adequately compensate for rape or other forms of sexual abuse. However, litigation has a preventive effect by making potential third-party defendants, and their insurance carriers, aware of their responsibility to reduce opportunities for rape to occur. And, for the individual plaintiff, demanding personal accountability of assailants and negligent third parties by bringing civil suit may help repair the damaged self-esteem and sense of powerlessness which often follow sexual assault. (Institute for the Study of Sexual Assault, 1983-1987)

The vast majority of rapes (87 percent) occurred to victims between the ages of 11 and 30. An examination of the age of the victim on a yearly basis shows the most vulnerable years to be from 13 to 26. (Russell, 1984, pp. 80-81)

The results of the study have additional implications for treatment and research. The extent of sexual victimization uncovered by the national survey suggests that clinicians should consider including questions about unwanted sexual activity in routine intake interviewing of women clients.... (Koss,1988, p. 22)

A woman can be raped at any age, from infancy to cronehood, but a feminist vocational expert analysis will be focused on the data which indicate the "most vulnerable years to be from 13 to 26 (Russell, 1984, pp. 80-81)," *because these are the years when vocational identity should be formed by attending high school and college and/or by entering the waged labor market.*

The vulnerable years for rape are true in marital rape patterns as well. Russell (1990) notes that "almost two-thirds of the women who were raped by their husbands (64 percent) were raped for the first time between the ages of thirteen and twenty-five" (1990, pp. 186-187).

Current theories of career choice for women do not adequately explain the vocational behavior of women since most of these theories are either based upon research done with men or with white women only.

Is it an accident that the average age (13 to 16 years) of inducement and/or extortion into prostitution also falls into the vulnerable years for rape?

Current theories of career choice for women do not adequately explain the vocational behavior of women since most of these theories are either based upon research done with men or with white women only. And none of these theories address the impact of rape on the vocational choices of women working in the waged and/or unwaged work worlds (Fitzgerald & Crites, 1980).

Vocational rehabilitation counselors and vocational experts would be well served to routinely inquire as to "unwanted sexual activity" while taking a woman's vocational history. Rapes which occur during the formation of a work identity may have long-lasting vocational implications. For example, in *Harriet's Story* we find the loss of an entire profession as an art historian and curator. This loss is directly related to Harriet's experience of rape and assault during her discovery of the profession, and her efforts to develop her skills and knowledge in the profession through work and school. And even though Harriet was able to complete her degree, she lost the profession: *I tried to go back into my field, but the flashbacks, the memories.*

And yet, I have found that taking a vocational history along with a woman's abuse history can have dramatic effects in the survivor's recovery process.

The only data I have been able to locate on this issue comes from my own work as a vocational rehabilitation counselor and from the co-researchers for this book. And yet, I have found that taking a vocational history along with a woman's abuse history can have dramatic effects in the survivor's recovery process. A therapist referred a client to me for "vocational blocks" which she and the client had been unable to resolve. Using the initial intake method of obtaining a vocational history along with an abuse history, the client and I uncovered a sexual assault which had taken place almost 20 years before, when the client was a young college woman. She had not mentioned this assault to her therapist because she had been told by a previous therapist that the assault was not an assault, not a rape. We then examined her vocational aspirations before and after the rape. The client and I concluded that the reason she had never finished college and stopped painting was because something inside her had died that day. That *something* was her creative impulse, her passion to work in the world. Twenty years later, she was still making do and getting by in the world of work. She went back to her therapist with this vital piece of information, and at last report, she is blooming in every level of her life, including her worklife (Murphy, 1992).

Just as women's work identities and work patterns cannot be fairly compared to men's work identities and work patterns, we cannot ignore ethnic and class issues within the category *woman*. As Klepfisz (1990) writes:

> I believe there is a far greater mixture and mix-up of education, class, and economic insecurity among women than feminists recognize....our movement has too often equated the issues of class and race, thereby obscuring the need for a separate analysis of each. One result has been an erasure of the white working-class experience. A white woman–and especially a Jew like myself–is usually assumed to be middle class, while a woman of color–especially Black, Hispanic or Native American–is usually assumed to be working-class or poor, which is often, but not inevitably, true. (pp. 16-17)

Therefore, since most of the data on the vocational consequences of rape will arise from research on college women because they are a relatively easy population to locate and because they are engaged in vocational identity formation, it will be the task of vocational counselors to pay attention to the complexities of class, race, educational levels, and participation in waged and unwaged work when providing services. And to the best of my knowledge, no research has yet been conducted on the work patterns of college women following acquaintance rape even though campus rape explodes every few years into the popular presses as a new and important issue.

Hine (1989), in her discussion of Black women's migration from South to North connects rape and work as follows:

> I believe that in order to understand this historical migratory trend we need to understand the noneconomic motives propelling Black female migration. I believe that many Black women quit the South out of a desire to achieve personal autonomy and to escape both from sexual exploitation from inside and outside their families and from the rape and threat of rape by white as well as Black males. To focus on the sexual and personal impetus for Black women's migration in the first several decades of the twentieth century neither dismisses nor diminishes the significance of economic motives....

Hine also notes the importance of the National Association of Colored Women's Clubs (NACW):

> Likewise, determination to save young, unskilled and unemployed Black women from having to bargain sex in exchange for food and shelter motivated some NACW members to establish boarding houses and domestic service training centers, such as the Phyllis Wheatley Homes, and Burrough's National Training School. (pp. 912-920)

I would go further than Hine and assert that rape and the desire to be free from rape are economic and vocational issues.

And just as I do not support the choice model of rape found in the rape paradigm, I do not subscribe to the choice model of vocational identity and development in women in some sort of equal opportunity approach. This is because I agree with Rhode (1990) that:

> Individual career choices often represent preconceptions about "women's work," which are shaped by cultural stereotypes, family and peer pressure, and the absence of alternative role models. Individual choices have also been constrained by unconscious discrimination and workplace structures. (pp. 170)

Therefore, I am not suggesting individual psychotherapy and vocational rehabilitation counseling as solutions to structural and system problems requiring political and social action. *Instead, I am suggesting that rape needs to be examined as a fundamental element in the constriction and suppression of women's work identities both on an individual level in counseling strategies and on a political level in making social policy to improve women's work lives.*

The connections between work and rape have not surfaced in civil sexual assault cases either. Out of the 150 cases summarized between 1983 and 1987 by the Institute For The Study of Sexual Assault, only two economists are listed under plaintiff's experts. Most of the experts used are psychologists, rape crisis counselors, psychiatrists, and security experts. The data do not reveal how the economists were used, but in personal injury cases, it is common to use economists in the assessment of lost earning capacity as well as in assessing future medical costs and other damages resulting from the injury. Vocational experts can either work with economists in developing hypotheticals regarding lost earning capacity or provide the number-crunching services themselves.

But in order to provide testimony for rape survivors, feminist vocational experts will need to become knowledgeable about Rape Trauma Syndrome (RTS) as well. Early research conducted in the 1970s indicated that rape may create the following symptoms: sleep and eating disorders, phobias, intrusive thoughts about the events, and flashbacks. Many victims were unable to return to work or to school (Boland, 1990a; Burgess & Holmstrom, 1985). Although RTS is generally considered to be a subcategory of PTSD, a current critical review of RTS indicates that more research is needed to determine if it is advantageous to conceptualize RTS as a variant of PTSD (Anderson, Frank, & Moss, 1991). Acceptance of RTS in the courts still varies widely from state to state and from case to case (Boland, 1990a). Therefore, the presentation of a lost earning capacity analysis based on RTS will require both courage and creativity on the part of vocational experts and attorneys in civil sexual assault cases.

Civil sexual assault cases are now being filed against apartment owners, assailants, employers of assailants, employers of plaintiff-victims, government entities, innkeepers, institutions, schools or care facilities, owners of public places, and common carriers (cab and bus companies) (Institute for the Study of Sexual Assault, 1983-1987; Minnesota Institute of Legal Education, 1990). Recoveries for damages range from $15,000 to $5,100,000.

Harriet's Story was placed prior to this chapter on civil sexual assault cases because her story allows for an examination of a potential civil sexual assault case against her assailant, a potential sexual harassment case (employment discrimination case) against her restaurant job employer, and a civil sexual assault case against her apartment owner/ manager. How an attorney would file these suits, and how the courts would sort them out, is not the purview of the vocational expert. It may be that only one suit would be filed, with the loss of Harriet's waitress job considered as part of damages Harriet sustained as a result of the psychological and physical injuries inflicted upon her by Phil. (Harriet was able to fend off the boss who demanded sex with her until she was repeatedly raped and beaten by Phil.) Then there's the complication of Harriet finding a rapist shot to death in the patio of her apartment. Harriet says: *I went into trauma.* This trauma, however, occurred after Phil had forcibly raped Harriet after minor gynecological surgery. Would Harriet have been as traumatized by the death of the rapist if she had not been raped by Phil?

This appears to be a case in which the rape shield law provisions will need to be used by the attorney, if only to simplify the case. Fortunately for the vocational expert, the task is not to prove that the rapes, the traumas, and the sexual harassment took place but that there are vocational consequences to these experiences resulting in lost wages and possible lost earning capacity. It is the prerogative of judges and juries to determine the facts of a case, while it is the task of the expert to provide specialized knowledge which will allow the fact finders to come to a correct determination (Massaro, 1985).

Therefore, this analysis will be based on the assumption that Harriet has a diagnosis of PTSD with features of RTS.

Harriet had a rich educational and work history at the time of her assault by Phil. She held a bachelor's degree and had been admitted to graduate school in art history. She had two jobs; clerical worker and waitress. Her job as a clerical worker provided her with entry into the occupation of curator in a museum, and her graduate school training insured maintenance of her position as well as advancement within the museum.

Harriet's birthdate is August 17, 1950 and her race is white. The date of injury will be based on the loss of Harriet's job at the museum on March 27, 1987. This leaves Harriet with a worklife expectancy of 22.4 years (Fredlund, 1986-1989).

Hypothetical #1: If Harriet had been able to maintain a position as a curator at the museum, rather than rehabilitating herself as a human services worker in a shelter for formerly battered women, what would her earnings have been? What earnings has she lost over her worklife expectancy? It is assumed that Harriet completed her graduate education by 6/30/87 and moved to full-time employment with a raise and an annual salary of $23,846 (U.S. Department of Labor, Bureau of Labor Statistics, 1990). This wage would have carried a 15% benefit ratio. The position at the shelter started at $15,000 annually with no benefits (U.S. Department of Labor, Bureau of Labor Statistics, 1990). As a curator, Harriet would have earned $623,547. As a human services worker, she would have earned $341,084. The loss over her 22.4 years of worklife is **$188,041 to $228,481** depending upon the discount rate.

Hypothetical #2: What are the lost wages and tips sustained by Harriet from when she lost her waitress job, 12/7/86, to 9/28/87 when she obtained another waitress job? If Harriet could have kept her original waitress job with an income level of $800 per month, she would have earned $8,800 during these 11 months. Since she could not, her loss is **$8,900**.

Hypothetical #3: What are Harriet's lost wages from the date of losing her curator job on 3/27/87 to date of trial on 2/3/90? It is assumed that Harriet continued working part-time until 6/30/87 when she went to a full-time position. Her earnings at the museum would have been $64,582. Harriet worked as a waitress (with another employer) starting on 9/28/87 making $12,000 annually with tips and wages (U.S. Department of Labor, Bureau of Labor Statistics, 1990-1991). Harriet earned approximately $10,000 as a waitress with her new employer. Harriet volunteered at the battered women's shelter for no pay until she obtained a staff position on 7/20/88 starting at $15,000 annually. She earned approximately $23,750. With her waitress and human services worker jobs Harriet earned $33,750, but if she had been able to keep her museum job she would have earned $64,582. Therefore, her loss is **$30,832**.

Since Harriet basically rehabilitated herself by working at a battered women's shelter as a human services worker, no vocational rehabilitation analysis is offered. Still, a vocational loss has occurred both financially and hedonically (i.e., deprivation of the pleasures of life). *Harriet's Story* is a recounting of her discovery of a work which engaged her passionately, fully. The loss of this work has a value above and beyond the lost earnings experienced by Harriet. Although the concept of hedonic damages is most frequently found in wrongful death cases, it can also be used to help assess damages for pain and suffering (Smith, 1988). Setting a dollar value on the pleasures of enjoyable work is probably as difficult as setting a dollar value on a human life, but as a vocational rehabilitation counselor, I have observed a lack of pleasure or passion for work as a common theme among my clients. Often, these clients have experienced abuse either as children and/or as adults. This is an area of expertise for vocational rehabilitationists which has scarcely been explored, let alone testified to in a civil sexual assault case. This promises to be fertile ground for speculation and controversy as more civil sexual assault cases are filed and the connections between work and rape become more sophisticated and better understood. For the purposes of demonstration, I will cite Magrowski's (1991) study which indicates that testimony is now being allowed in the courts for the loss of an occupation for which one has prepared and that an average hedonic award for persons with an occupational history was **$209,971.40**.

Harriet's expenses for psychotherapy to recover from her assault(s) should also be included in any damage awards. Future psychotherapeutic treatment and vocational rehabilitation counseling services should also be projected into the damage award calculations even though Harriet was able to continue working as a waitress and in an agency for formerly battered women and their children. Figures for these expenses are speculative on my part since Harriet did not tell me how much money she had spent on psychotherapy after her assaults. Harriet's work in a shelter for formerly battered women and their children also involved group counseling for staff members and can be considered a sort of employee assistance program benefit. Conservatively, I will estimate these counseling services at a value of **$3,600.**

But even if Harriet were to be awarded any of these amounts, nothing, not a penny of any of these monies, can make up for the assaults on Harriet's sexuality, her being, and the loss of a life's work.

An argument can be made that Harriet's level of work in an agency for battered women and their children is an intensive, self-procured vocational rehabilitation effort equivalent to graduate work in women's studies on violence against women. The estimated cost of such a program (resident tuition, books and supplies) at a state college or university is $3,450 (University of Nevada, 1990-1991). This does not include a living allowance while attending school full-time. Vocational rehabilitation counseling and psychotherapy during her two years of graduate work in women's studies or if Harriet should need assistance in leaving the protected work environment of the shelter setting is estimated at **$5,400.**

But even if Harriet were to be awarded any of these amounts, nothing, not a penny of any of these monies, can make up for the assaults on Harriet's sexuality, her being, and the loss of a life's work. What the money can do is send a message: Harriet, like all victims of war, deserves war reparations.

You know how I feel? When I got the money, I felt as though I were being paid for sex. I felt like a whore.

—from *Marlene's Story*

marlene's story*

Both the physical and sexual abuse started when I was an infant. My father and mother seemed to take turns. I have an older sister, a half sister. I had a younger sister, but she died. She was 13 years old when she died. My father was driving the car in his maniacal way and we went over a cliff, and she died. I was 15 and I still have scars on my legs, three compressed vertebrae in my back. I had to wear a back brace for a year. My father was severely injured. I don't want to talk about this now. I'm not done. I've not said good-bye to her yet.

I'm 41 years old, and I think being abused early in life teaches one a sort of behavior that says people can do things to my physical body, and I can do nothing about it. I cannot acknowledge it; I cannot proclaim any outrage. I don't feel like a human being. Other people are human beings, but I'm sort of like a dog. People can kick me, abuse me, and I haven't the right to stand up for myself.

The first thing I remember is being an infant and my father toying with my genitals. I didn't have the muscle control to move my hands and arms to get his hands away from me. I didn't have the intellectual capacity to even understand what was happening. I just knew it was against the rule of my being.

Then there were the stories of how I was found in my crib with straw under my fingernails. My older sister confessed to doing it, but then recanted. My mother and grandmother still talk about how they extracted the straw, "Oh, we used to take tweezers and pull the straw out. We could never figure out how it got there."

My mother burned me with cigarettes. People started asking her about all the bruises and burns they could see on me in the family photo albums, and so she showed me all the pictures one day, and then she burned them. After that she only hurt me where

---

*In her own words.

it wouldn't show. This is hard to tell. She used pliers on my clitoris, my vagina. Clothespins. As I got past toddler stage, I resisted. So then she quit leaving marks. She collected coat hangers. She unwound them and when she had a dozen, she twisted them together and beat me with them. She hit me on my legs, torso, and arms. She was so seductive. She'd promise to be nice. I'd fall for it every time. Then she'd burn me or hit me or something. I hit her once after my sister died, and she smiled. It was scary. She did the wire hanger thing to my little sister, too, before she died. She never did anything in front of my older sister. It was all in private.

My father? He used his hand. No wire hangers for him. He killed my dog in front of me. He said there were too many women and niggers in the world. We should be thinned out like cattle. He would tell me stories of how we should be killed. Lined up and shot. Put out on a boat to sea. Starved to death. Maybe it was because my mother's side of the family was partly African-American. It was a big secret. I was supposed to pass as white.

When I was eight or nine years old, my cousin raped me. He was probably 15. My father found out somehow. My mother knew, too. I heard them talking. My sister and I used to hold onto each other and sing songs real loud so we wouldn't have to hear our parents yelling when they fought. Then suddenly, I had a room by myself and my older sister was with my little sister. My mother said it was because I made such a big fuss about the rape.

And then my father came into my room at night. Yes, it was full intercourse. Yes, I think it was because my mother sent him. Pain? You ask about pain? Excruciating pain became part of my life. I went to school with it. Actually, it's hard for me to make sense about something being painful. I have a difficult time paying attention to pain even now. I'm in deep trouble with my left shoulder. I was in a car accident a couple of years ago. I "pooh-poohed" the whole thing. Now I've got tendonitis, bursitis, a frozen shoulder. I have to have surgery. I'm not connected to my body. My doctors tell me pain is a signal. I don't receive it.

I was not allowed to go to college. My father didn't believe in education for women. He wanted to pull my sister and me out of elementary school but he couldn't. He told me to not trust my teachers or anything I read in books. I couldn't study at home. I got by with C's. My sister was failing the seventh grade when she died. Neither of my parents graduated from high school, but I did. Then I wasn't allowed to leave home until my mother figured out the perfect job for me. I became an airline stewardess. Nineteen and one half was the earliest the airline would take girls, and so I went from my home in Kansas City, Missouri to New York City. I was terrified.

My mother wanted me to be a flight attendant. I didn't want to. I wanted music. I wanted art. I was told by the school counselors to become a secretary. I flew for two years, and I began to understand that I needed help, that something was wrong. I had nightmares. I couldn't relate to people. I was thin, emotionally thin.

I met a psychotherapist at a party. At first, I was turned-off to him because he came on to me, but he presented a kind of reality to me, a kindness I had never experienced. I became a patient in his group. He was one of a group of psychologists with doctorates from Harvard and UCLA, places like that. I wasn't able to make all the appointments, the group-therapy meetings, because I was flying. I was gone a lot. I didn't have much control over my schedule.

The pressure began. Subtle, you know. Maybe I should stop flying. Then it was my reading. I loved to read. I subscribed to Ramparts Magazine, Newsweek, Harpers. They said they had a therapy superior to Carl Rogers or Alder, or even Freud because, unlike Rogers, Alder, or Freud, they worked together. This way they could overcome the limitations of any one person's skill level. This was in the early 1970s. They were a cult, but I didn't know it. They didn't look like a cult.

Anyway, I stopped my reading. I took a medical leave of absence. One of my assignments was to have sex, to have intercourse at least once per week. So I had sex with other patients who were also given these sex assignments as well as with the six male therapists. I started getting vaginal infections. Now I think it was resistance, internal resistance. I begged the therapists, ``It's like being raped.'' I got yeast infections. The doctors told me to get off the pill. I got an IUD. It perforated my uterus and I was hospitalized. So, I went on medical leave. I never flew full-time after that.

Then it was decided that I should live with other patients in a house. Eventually, I lived with a man who was also a patient. He was told to support me. He had money. I didn't know about this until the class action lawsuit was filed. I lived with him because I was told I needed to do so for my mental health.

By 1973 or 1974, I had become a group leader. Under the cult's direction, I went to a community college where I got a state license as a psychiatric technician. I was told that this would allow me to lead groups, and if I were good enough I might even get paid. I had more than 24 clients at one point. Later I found that what I was doing was illegal and that the center was billing for my services at the psychologists' rates.

I went to the university extension in art and design on my savings. I began to have anxiety attacks in class when I realized I could do as well as anyone else. I was told to quit. I quit. I wanted to get a B.A. from an alternative degree program. There was another woman in the group who was doing it, and she was told to not talk to me.

After the fifth year I started doing public relations for them. They were famous guys. They had published books and I got them on Good Morning America, the Today Show, the Dinah Shore Show. I got them on the college lecture circuit, into magazines and newspapers. That's what I was doing when the bubble burst. It all exploded in a week. There were 600 patients in the community or cult in Denver, hundreds more on the East Coast, even Canada. Poof! It was all gone. Ten years with them from 1970 to 1980. It vanished.

In the last year, I had started to say something was wrong. I was punished for it. I was kicked out of my group. Responsibility and recognition was taken away from me. I was screamed at for hours about my disloyalty. Then the psychologists turned on each other. It was all over. The man who supported me left. I had hives, nightmares, herpes. I was still sleeping with whomever my first therapist directed me to. My body started shaking and wouldn't stop. I didn't have a job or a car. Then the man, who had supported me, gave me a car.

With this car, I sold plants. I swallowed my pride, and I bought a car load of plants. I drove to office buildings and sold them. With the money I got, I bought more. I built it up into a little business. I did it for three years. I figured out that I made 50,000 in tax-free dollars one year. I got my bachelor's degree then, from 1981 to 1983, at a school in Denver which gives credit for work and life experiences. Then I stopped selling plants. I was ashamed. I wanted to be more professional. The business got beyond me, more than I could manage. I knew how to do it in the only the most elementary way. I didn't know how to do the books. I couldn't manage.

Why would I give up a $50,000 annual income? I have two thoughts. First, the business was never real to me. I couldn't make it real. I was ashamed. Secondly, I wanted to go somewhere else. I thought, "Well, if I can do this, I can do anything." But actually, I've never worked consistently since, and I've never made that much money again. I'm shaking. Putting together my worklife with my abuse history—I've never done this before. Now the connections seem obvious. I think I cannot commit to anything, you see. If I'm not anywhere, then I'm safe. Right? Exactly. They can't catch me. They can't burn me if I'm liquid, and I move.

Then there's the lawsuit. Twenty-five of us sued. It was a class action suit. We won. Psychological malpractice. I got a big chunk of money, but it's gone now. It was less than what my earnings would have been if I had kept flying. Workers' Compensation? No, that was never brought up. Sure I worked for them. One year they paid me almost $5,000. Another year I made $480.00. Sure I was both a patient and an employee. No, no one ever talked to me about being a worker. You know how I feel? When I got the money, I felt as though I were being paid for sex. I felt like a whore.

I'd like to study sexism. How it works. I want to get a doctorate. I guess I'm still trying to figure out how to be a professional, something I'm not ashamed of.

nine

---

the use of vocational experts in incest, pornography, and prostitution cases

Nowhere is woman treated according to the merit of her work, but rather as a sex. It is therefore almost inevitable that she should pay for her right to exist, to keep a position in whatever line, with sex favors. Thus it is merely a question of degree whether she sells herself to one man, in or out of marriage, or to many men. Whether our reformers admit it or not, the economic and social inferiority of woman is responsible for prostitution. (Goldman, 1970, p. 20)

People hurt other people in many ways that are not against the law. To have a "cause of action" means that there is a law against what happened, so one can sue. The victims do not have to first fight about whether they are permitted to sue or not, the way women now, without the Ordinance, have to fight when they want to stop being hurt by pornography. With a cause of action, one only has to prove that what the law provides for you has happened to you. The Ordinance provides five such possibilities for suit: for coercion into pornography, for having pornography forced on you, for being assaulted because of particular pornography, for defamation through pornography, and for trafficking in pornography. (Dworkin & MacKinnon, 1988, p. 41)

Perhaps *the* challenge of the 1990s, for the vocational expert, will be the ability to prepare cases for the civil courts in which the plaintiffs are victims used in prostitution and pornography. Many of these victims will have complex abuse histories. And although not all prostitution survivors are incest victims and not all incest victims are used in prostitution, the connections between childhood sexual abuse and prostitution are too consistent and all too pervasive to be overlooked (Campagna & Poffenberger, 1988). Pornography appears to play a key role in all forms of abuse and cannot be separated from child abuse (Russell, 1988).

Therefore, just as prostitution cannot be separated from pornography, incest cannot be separated from prostitution.

Therefore, just as prostitution cannot be separated from pornography, incest cannot be separated from prostitution. And prostitution cannot be separated from women's oppression no matter what its form. *Marlene's Story* is placed in front of this chapter not because she is defined as a prostitute, but because she says: *When I got the money, I felt as though I were being paid for sex. I felt like a whore.* This theme echoes in the co-researchers' stories. *Grace's Story: I felt like I was whoring for kisses; Anita's Story: Feeling like a prostitute, feeling used, feeling degraded, feeling humiliated.* The co-researchers teach us that patriarchal efforts to separate women from each other, particularly "respectable" women from women perceived as prostitutes, have failed.

Abused women understand prostitution as the center of the rape paradigm without the need for any academic or erudite explanations (Liss, 1980).

The groundbreaking work of Dworkin and MacKinnon (1988) challenges the very foundation of the rape paradigm and opens the way for women used in systems of prostitution, including pornography, to sue in the civil courts.

Dworkin and MacKinnon (1988) are not promoting some new wrinkle in obscenity law but the right to sue in civil court. No criminal penalties are involved. The principle here is, "The status quo must become too costly for the dominant society to bear" (p. 46-47).

Pornography is defined by Dworkin and MacKinnon (1988) as sex discrimination:

> Through its production, pornography is a traffic in female sexual slavery. Through its consumption, pornography further institutionalizes a subhuman, victimized, second-class status for women by conditioning orgasm to sex inequality. When men use pornography, they experience in their bodies that one-sided sex-sex between a person and a thing-is sex, that sexual use is sex, sexual abuse is sex, sexual domination is sex. Pornography makes sexism sexy. It is a major way that gender hierarchy is enjoyed and practiced. Pornography is a sacred, secret codebook that has both obscured and determined women's lives. There laid bare is misogyny's cold heart: sexual violation enjoyed, power and powerlessness as sex. Pornography links sexual use and abuse with gender inequality by equating them: the inequality between women and men is both what is sexy about pornography and what is sex discriminatory about it. (pp. 46-47)

Another reason for selecting *Marlene's Story* to open this chapter is that her story of childhood sexual and physical torture and the subsequent abuse experienced in a cult has an eerie similarity to *Laura's Story*, which is a story of incest and a lifetime of prostitution. Even though the details are different, how can Marlene's experience be considered qualitatively different from Laura's? The men in *Marlene's Story* had Ph.D.s and had written books, but they behaved like pimps by using Marlene to run counseling groups (illegally) and by charging top rates for the service while paying Marlene very little (Giobbe, 1990; Silbert & Pines, 1982). Further, Marlene was expected to deliver sexual services to male therapists upon demand, and to have sex with other male patients as directed by her main therapist/pimp. Since Marlene was perceived as a victim of medical malpractice by the courts, she was able to file a lawsuit in the civil courts and collect damages. Therefore, the difference between Laura and Marlene is that Marlene could sue and Laura could not.

Dworkin and MacKinnon's (1988) work means that, if she were in the right jurisdiction and the Ordinance had not been rejected, Laura could sue. *Laura's Story* includes Laura's use in the making of hardcore pornography known as loops. Loops are shown in quarter booths in sex shops across the country. In the legal brothels of Nevada, prostitutes are expected to purchase pornographic materials to be used as part of the sexual service offered to customers (Ryan, 1990).

Both Laura and Marlene have a basis for filing a suit against their childhood sexual and physical abuse perpetrators (or in Laura's case, the estate of the perpetrator). Such suits are being filed in the civil courts and damages collected (Institute for the Study of Sexual Assault, 1983-1987). This assumes, of course, that perpetrators have something with which to pay damages, but such suits may also serve as part of the recovery process for some survivors regardless of actual damages collected.

Finally, both Marlene and Laura have arrived at their fourth decades without a transferable skills and knowledge base which would allow them to face the future with dignity. The childhood abuse destroyed their ability to get the education they wanted and deserved, and their abuse as adults disallowed any opportunity to develop work identities in any meaningful work. Laura comes from an affluent, white family background and Marlene from a poor family hiding its African-American heritage. And yet the abuse histories of these two women bind them together in a commonality of vocational positioning which could never have been predicted by the conventional wisdom of vocational experts. The point is that the hypotheticals developed in Marlene's case would not differ greatly in a case developed for Laura.

For example, a case filed against the child physical abuse and sexual perpetrators for both Laura and Marlene would involve discussion of the Child Sexual Abuse Accommodation Syndrome developed by Roland Summit. Summit (1983) describes the five phases as: 1) engagement; 2) sexual interaction; 3) secrecy; 4) disclosure; and 5) suppression.

Summit (1983) also describes five phases which are: 1) secrecy; 2) helplessness; 3) entrapment and accommodation; 4) delayed, conflicted, and unconvincing disclosure; and 5) retraction. Summit's model is named Child Sexual Abuse Accommodation Syndrome.

The childhood abuse destroyed their ability to get the education they wanted and deserved, and their abuse as adults disallowed any opportunity to develop work identities in any meaningful work.

This model has had little acceptance from the courts since testimony based on his syndrome is seen as usurping the function of the judge and jury because the syndrome evidence is used to prove (with children) that the sexual abuse occurred. However, the models can be used to explain certain behaviors of children (e.g., recantation or delay in reporting the abuse) (Boland, 1990b).

Such explanations might prove very useful for vocational experts when constructing hypotheticals for adult incest survivors who are now claiming damages to their earning capacities. Statute of limitation issues may differ from state to state, but some states have disallowed such defenses (as statue of limitations) by ruling familial sexual abuse as a cumulative injury which does not stop until the date of the last abuse (Boland, 1990b). The Institute for the

Study of Sexual Assault (ISSA) case summaries from 1983-1987 show awards for such cases ranging from $27,000 to $10,000,000.

Although the pornography as sex discrimination ordinance, as proposed by Dworkin and MacKinnon (1988), has not been implemented in the United States, one of the cases summarized by ISSA (1983-1987) contains, within the facts of the case, the forcing of the nine year-old plaintiff to watch pornography and be photographed for pornography. The legal theories in this case included sexual assault and battery, negligence, and gross negligence. The assailant was the mother's former live-in boyfriend, and the settlement, which was paid, was for $60,000. Therefore, the principles espoused by Dworkin and MacKinnon are already successfully implemented in civil sexual assault cases. The difficulty seems to lie in the unwillingness of our society to extend protection and rights to the most vulnerable of women–women and girls used in prostitution.

Marlene's case will be analyzed in terms of damage to her earning capacity. Childhood physical and sexual abuse and their impact on vocational capacity for Marlene will be presented. Impairment to vocational capacity resulting from injuries sustained as an adult would be presented as separate from the childhood abuse experiences. This is because rape shield laws, which construct the prior sexual history of a victim as irrelevant, will not permit the connecting of childhood abuse experiences to adult abuse experiences (Largen, 1988).

Marlene's sexual and physical abuse was inflicted upon her by both parents. Both parents also limited her vocational development. Marlene's father reluctantly allowed his daughters to attend school, but only because he was forced to do so by law. Marlene and her sister were not allowed to study at home. Despite being tortured, beaten, raped, and threatened, Marlene managed to graduate from high school. Marlene's parents did not allow her to consider college. She was also not allowed to work after high school until she was nineteen and one-half years old. This was the age airlines accepted young women for flight attendant positions. Marlene became a flight attendant as directed and planned by her mother. Marlene never wanted to be an airline stewardess. Even though Marlene said: *I wanted music. I wanted art.* She worked as a flight attendant from 1970 to 1974 when she was forced to stop working by the cult and work only for them at minimum or no wages. After 10 years of being abused inside the cult, Marlene was awarded damages for lost earnings, medical expenses for psychiatric treatment, reimbursement for psychotherapy payments to the cult, and reimbursement for loss of monies due to being coerced to purchase an office condominium.

Marlene was further coerced into obtaining a psychiatric technician license by the cult. She also took art and design courses and this knowledge was exploited by the cult. She managed to obtain a B.A. from an alternative degree program which gave credit for work and life experiences after leaving the cult, but she was not able to empower herself by using her education to advance her worklife. Marlene did work sporadically after leaving the cult, but was unable to sustain employment or self-employment. Marlene says she earned $50,000 one year in her plant business but left it because she was ashamed. She was probably also in trouble with the IRS since she hadn't paid her taxes. She says she didn't know enough to handle the business properly.

Marlene's future earning capacity was considered to be impaired by her psychiatrist and her attorneys, but this was not addressed in her damage award. And although Marlene was an employee as well as a patient of the cult, no mention was ever made to her about an employment discrimination lawsuit for sex discrimination or a workers' compensation claim for an on-the-job injury. In other words, Marlene's identity as a worker was not taken seriously enough to assist her with examining the vocational impairment to her future earning capacity nor in providing her with monies which would allow her to recover vocationally through a process of vocational rehabilitation. That Marlene could have used such assistance is evidenced by her having lived for the past 10 years on her settlement without advancing herself vocationally. The settlement is now gone. As Marlene says: *I think I cannot commit to anything. If I'm not anywhere, then*

I'm safe. Right? Exactly. They can't catch me. They can't burn me if I'm liquid, and I move.

It should be pointed out that the amount of Marlene's damage award was less than the amount of money she could have made working as a flight attendant during the 10 years of her abusive experiences within the cult. In order to stretch this money over 10 years, Marlene has lived frugally.

Marlene's future earning capacity was considered to be impaired by her psychiatrist and her attorneys, but this was not addressed in her damage award.

Vocational experts are not attorneys, and so I am not suggesting that the information developed below meets legal standards for statute of limitation issues, rape shield law provisions, or the appropriate arenas for the bringing of suits. For example, sex discrimination lawsuits are generally brought under employment law provisions, but there are situations where such suits may surface in workers' compensation settings. In Marlene's case, there may have been legal reasons for only filing a medical malpractice suit and no employment discrimination suit. In any event, Marlene's future earning capacity was not addressed and it should have been wherever the lawsuit originated.

Marlene's birthdate is September 20, 1950. She self-identifies as white, but also has an African-American heritage. Governmental life expectancy and worklife expectancy statistical tables separate whites and African-Americans. In Marlene's case, the worklife expectancy of 28.2 years is the same if she is perceived as a white woman or as an African-American woman. This worklife expectancy is dated from Marlene's graduation from college at the age of 24 years.

With projected life expectancy statistics, Marlene's life expectancy as a white woman is 36.9 years (or 77.9) but as an African-American woman it is 35.7 years (or 76.7). Life expectancy statistics are drawn from the National Center for Health Statistics and worklife expectancy data are from the U.S. Department of Labor Bureau of Labor Statistics (Fredlund, 1986-1989).

Marlene's plant business is not included in any analyses because of the quixotic nature of the enterprise which did not lead to any sustained employment or income.

Hypothetical #1: If Marlene had not been abused by her parents and had been allowed to study during grade school and high school and continued on into college in art and design, what would have been the costs of her college education? What would her earnings as a designer be as of 1/2/92 (date of trial)? It is assumed that Marlene would have received only partial support from her parents during her college years at a state university. This support would have taken the form of college tuition and books. Marlene would have worked part-time under work study programs and earned some scholarship monies. The total cost to the parents for tuition and books would have been $6,750 (University of Nevada, 1990-1991). Over 28.2 years as a designer with a starting salary of around $15,000 annually and benefits at a 15% ratio, Marlene would have earned $575,851 (United States Department of Labor, Bureau of Labor Statistics, 1972-1973).

Hypothetical #2: If Marlene had worked as a flight attendant over her 28.2 years of worklife expectancy, what would her earnings have been? With a starting wage of $12,904 and fringe benefits at the 15% ratio, Marlene would have earned $422,185. Therefore, if Marlene had been able to pursue her own wishes she would have earned $153,666 more as a designer than as a flight attendant. In adjusting such a damage award for the discount rate, the range is between $85,898 and $112,939.

Hypothetical #3: Marlene pursued her art education by taking classes while she was in the cult. She provided design services to her psychologists/employers in the cult when they built and furnished their new homes. If she had been paid for these services, what would she have earned? It is assumed that Marlene could have charged $15.00 per hour for her services as a designer and that she provided 200 hours of design work (United States Department of Labor, Bureau of Labor Statistics, 1972-1973). Marlene would have earned $3,000.

This exploitation of Marlene appears to have also destroyed Marlene's last hopes of becoming a designer. Therefore, noneconomic or hedonic damages for the loss of this long-sought vocational goal appears to be appropriate whether it is filed against Marlene's parents or against the cult. Citing Magrowski (1991) again, such damages have ranged between $27,095 and $209,917.

Hypothetical #4: Marlene says she wants to study sexism. Is this a feasible vocational rehabilitation plan? What is the cost of the vocational rehabilitation effort including counseling, education, transportation, and a living allowance during the rehabilitation effort? The basic assumption for any rehabilitation effort is that a person can benefit from it. In rehabilitation parlance, this is referred to as "feasibility."

Marlene's feasibility is highly problematic since, in my vocational expert opinion, Marlene's vocational potential has been destroyed by her life experiences of abuse. This is evidenced by Marlene's inability to advance vocationally in spite of the passage of 10 years since the settlement of her psychological malpractice case. Marlene could probably attend school, and even graduate, but her chances for obtaining employment are probably zero. The ability to function academically is certainly an aspect of vocational functioning, but so is the ability to interact socially, and this is what Marlene has lost. In short, Marlene has never been enculturated into a normal worklife. Her abuse experiences have contaminated the world of work for her.

In comparison, the development of a life care plan for Marlene is also problematic and more difficult to justify than for Laura, for example, because Laura is in continual danger of self-murder. Therefore, although no vocational rehabilitation plan for Marlene will be presented, the issue is raised to underscore the need for new vocational rehabilitation strategies and new legal strategies designed to assist women like Marlene in healing every aspect of their lives, including their work lives. Marlene is one of those people who fall and fall and fall between the cracks and past the safety net.

Perhaps a clue to Marlene's dilemma can be found in the recovery processes used by Harriet and by Anita. Both of these co-researchers used the formerly battered women's shelter movement to rehabilitate themselves. Marlene's wish to study sexism should perhaps not be constructed as women's studies coursework or degree programs, but instead as a form of activism and study such as Harriet and Anita experienced in their recoveries. The vocational rehabilitative function of shelter and rape crisis center settings for survivors has never been studied in any systematic way even though volunteers and staff for these agencies are drawn from survivors.

Not all survivors have the emotional strength to face the daily crisis work presented in shelters and rape crisis centers. Therefore, my recommendation would be that Marlene start out by volunteering in such an agency. This would give her complete control over how much she could tolerate while allowing her to undergo a process of work hardening and work enculturation in an environment uniquely supportive of her. Perhaps a life care plan for Marlene might look very similar to the arrangements in *Rhonda's Story*. Rhonda worked as a volunteer. She was unable to tolerate the world of work because of her experience of abuse. Marlene might have a better chance than Rhonda in that she does have more education and she is not in the advanced stages of alcoholism. The dignity in making a contribution to society as a productive worker cannot be overlooked as a rehabilitation strategy, even if this work is unpaid.

Laura's case is based on the notion that Laura could file a civil sexual assault suit against her grandfather's estate. If the extension of civil rights to prostituted women comes to fruition in the 1990s, perhaps a similar case could be filed against the people who used Laura in pornography and prostitution.

The trial date is arbitrarily chosen as March 3, 1992, and it is assumed that Laura's recent memory of the abuse will allow her to file suit within statute of limitation considerations in her state. Her date of birth is July 24, 1951. Her race is white. The date of injury is cumulative extending over a 10-month period ending on 12/2/55. The date(s) of injury in a case based on harm caused by pornography and/or prostitution could possibly change the calculations presented as in the case against Laura's grandfather, but the cases are the same in conceptualization.

Hypothetical #1: The childhood torture and sexual assault experienced by Laura before the age of four years old

---

Laura is finding it increasingly difficult to sustain the 14-hour shifts required at the legal brothel where she is now used as a prostitute.

---

prevented Laura from obtaining any coherent education and led directly to a life in prostitution. Her assailant used pornography and instructed Laura in posing for pornography even though no actual films were made.

The assumptions are that Laura has been diagnosed with PTSD and finds she experiences severe intrusive thoughts and memories, including commands to kill herself (Neland, undated). Laura has also been diagnosed with Multiple Personality Disorder (MPD).

Laura has undertaken heroic efforts to free herself from drug and alcohol addiction. She has also undertaken heroic efforts to come to terms with her recently remembered childhood abuse through therapy and group work in the local battered women's shelter.

Laura is finding it increasingly difficult to sustain the 14-hour shifts required at the legal brothel where she is now used as a prostitute. Laura's earnings as a prostitute (legal or illegal) cannot be included in this analysis because prostitution meets no test of the development of transferable skills which could be used in another occupation. In other words, like slavery, prostitution does not allow for the development of a recognized earning capacity. And even if prostitution could be constructed as an occupation, the social stigma of prostitution undermines Laura's credibility in applying for jobs in the waged labor market.

Vocational evaluation, including physical tolerance evaluation and psychometric testing, indicate that due to concentration difficulties, Laura has poor to zero chances in ever obtaining any employment and/or sustaining it for the rest of her worklife expectancy, which is 28.9 years if we use a hypothetical age of 24 years as Laura's entry into the waged labor market after completing college (Fredlund, 1986-1989).

Based on Laura's interest in writing and film or photography, I have selected photojournalist as the occupation she might have chosen for herself if she had not been tortured by her grandfather. In life care planning cases where there is no work history (as in the wrongful death of infants), the vocational expert looks to the parents' occupations in order to determine what level of achievement might be reasonably expected if the injury had not taken place. Laura's father did not go to college, but he was a successful banker. Laura's mother had attended college and she volunteered in charity functions as part of her upper class social obligations. Therefore, I felt safe in suggesting Laura as a photojournalist with two or three years of college or more. In the mid-1970s, journalists' had annual starting salaries of $6,818 with benefits included (United States Department of Labor, Bureau of Labor Statistics, 1972-1973). If Laura had been able to enter into this occupation, she would have earned $227,135, as a conservative figure. The recommended damage award would range between **$129,715 to $168,918** depending upon the discount rate.

Although Magrowski's (1991) study indicates that the average hedonic or noneconomic award for individuals who have not developed occupations is only **$27,917**, it should also be recalled that hedonic awards have ranged between **$500,000 to $3.5 million.** Laura's abuse experience and its results are so traumatic that it would be my speculation that any hedonic award to Laura would be on the high end of the scale.

A life care plan for Laura would focus on independent living skill development which would allow her to live without the threat of self-murder. Since recovery is an intellectual as well as a psychological process, Laura should also be encouraged to nurture her continuing interest in creative writing (Belenky, Clinchy, Goldberger, & Tarule, 1986).

As we discovered with Marlene, new rehabilitation strategies are needed to assist survivors like Laura. At the present time, the only agency which could address Laura's unique needs is the Council For Prostitution Alternatives (CPA) in Portland, Oregon. This agency estimates that their services, which include aggressive manipulation of community resources such as food stamps, free food programs, welfare, and medical assistance; counseling for Multiple Personality Disorder and PTSD survivors; support groups for prostitution survivors; advocacy in the courts and other bureaucracies; and housing-are at an incredibly low cost of approximately $3,000 per year per prostitution survivor! The agency presently serves 75 women per year (Neland, undated).

Obviously, not all prostitution survivors will be able to use this agency, but CPA does provide a model for life care planning for prostitution survivors. This agency, like shelters for formerly battered women and rape crisis centers, also draws from prostitution survivors for volunteers and staff. Therefore, a life care plan for Laura might look a great deal like the one suggested for Marlene, with volunteer work as part of the rehabilitation strategy.

Instead, she told me about her real injury. The pain and grief which was corroding her insides, her soul. Her back throbbed with it. She refused the drugs. She wanted her pain. It was all she had left.

–from Janet's Story

janet's story*

We drove the Los Angeles basin together in my little Honda with the air conditioning, down the Long Beach Freeway out to the Pasadena, and back again down the San Diego. We were grateful to be inside with the light gray upholstery and the blasting, frigid air while the sun burned the visible smog and the concrete of the freeway scorched the very sky.

We ran from our cocoon into buildings housing private trade and business colleges and more cold air. We shivered as the dampness under our arms and our waistbands dried. We reversed the process after each school visit, drying out again in the car.

We were looking for a school, an experience. Something which would bring her back into life again. She had a back injury. She couldn't stand at the drill press all day long anymore. I had tested her. She was bright. She had a brain. I was grateful her math levels were above the national average of sixth grade. Her reading levels were even better. So, computerized bookkeeping? Word processing? Conventional, but appropriate for an injured worker who needed light and sedentary work now. Maybe computerized drafting?

She limped grudgingly behind me all day long as we moved from car to building and back again. We sat in front of desks with admissions counselors behind them. We took tours, but when we got back in the car we didn't talk about the schools at all. Instead, she told me about her real injury. The pain and grief which was corroding her insides, her soul. Her back throbbed with it. She refused the drugs. She wanted her pain. It was all she had left.

"She was only 12, my pretty little daughter. She was so good in school. Straight A's in math and English. She walked to school every day. It was only six blocks from our house. All the kids did. No busing for my kids. It was the Catholic school, you know. All

---

*As told by the author.

the girls wore white blouses, plaid skirts, and matching navy blue sweaters, when it was cold.'' She twisted the straps on her purse.

''He took her right off the street, somewhere between St. Mary's School and our house, at eight o'clock in the morning! In the morning! We reported her missing when she didn't come home from school. I didn't [know], and my husband didn't know, she hadn't ever got [sic] to school because we both work.'' When she said, ''husband'' her face changed. A rage as cold as the air conditioning blast swept through our small space as I changed lanes, watched green signs for our exit, wondered how I was going to make a vocational rehabilitation plan out of this.

She straightened her knees, moving restlessly in the passenger seat. ''He had her all day and all night. The detective said she didn't die until the next morning. He tortured her. She was only 12, you know. She looked 16 maybe, but she was only 12. He used a knife on her. Raped her, too. The detective showed us the photographs and the reports. He wasn't supposed to, but he did. I had to see it. I had to know.''

And so it went, one long middle part of the day. Janet and I drove the L.A. freeway system and we remembered her daughter together. ''Was the guy caught?'' I asked. ''Oh, yeah. He was some guy from Kansas. Been in town a few weeks, staying with his brother. His brother turned him in when he got home from a vacation. There was blood all over the walls of the apartment. The guy's been in jail and they put him away for a few years, not many.''

Her words flowed over us in liquid ice, cold blood. No inflection, just a freezing passion of remembrance. We stayed there together, in that grieving. The excursions to the schools were just commas, semicolons in our dialogue. I listened. I asked questions. I listened.

At the end of the day she said, ''I'll do the computerized drafting.''

''Okay,'' I said. ''We can set that up with the insurance company.'' We never spoke of her daughter again.

ten

---

the use of vocational experts in wrongful death cases

White women (including Hispanic women) comprise the majority of intimate femicide victims. While white women comprise the majority of victims (60.44%), African-American women are disproportionately represented (37.12%). Forty-one Native American women and 41 Asian women were victims of intimate femicide. Further analysis of these data indicate that most of these killings were intraracial. (Stout, 1991, p. 3)

If a woman is going to die from an injury at work, she's probably going to be murdered. Statistics show that 42% of the deaths suffered by women on the job in this country between 1980 and 1985 were homicides....only 12% of the occupational fatalities among men were listed as homicides. The murders of women generally are the result of a crime, such as robbery, and involve the exchange of money and night employment. Of the victims, 41% worked in retail and 20% in the service industries. (Bell, 1991, p. 17)

Seiden summed up Mickey's behavior as ''exquisitely targeted sadism'' pointing out that by forcing Francine to burn her books he had forced her to destroy herself- what Sieden called ''her personhood''—since it was in school that she had ''begun to feel like a person for the first time in her life.'' (McNulty, pp. 211-212)

Wrongful death haunts the rehabilitation counselor in the stories of the survivors, the family members who bring both their injuries and their grief to the process. *Janet's Story* is an example of how a wrongful death can be a greater injury to the survivor than the presenting industrial injury.

Vocational experts, by contrast, are called upon to examine the lives of the deceased and their survivors. The loss of rehabilitative potential is the issue here, not the rehabilitation process itself. The story of Francine and Mickey Hughes becomes a rehabilitation story only because of the remarkable efforts of Francine Hughes.

Francine Hughes had to kill her husband to get off welfare and go to work.

The reason we know the story of *The Burning Bed* is because Francine killed Mickey Hughes. If Mickey had killed Francine, there would have been no best-selling book and no television movie (Stout, 1991). In vocational rehabilitation terminology, the Francine Hughes story could be constructed as a rehabilitation story. That is, Francine Hughes had to kill her husband to get off welfare and go to work. In rehabilitation parlance, a person who develops her or his own rehabilitation plan is said to have developed a *self-procured rehabilitation plan*. Meaning, a person who is so determined and so creative she rehabilitates herself, without the assistance of professionals.

Francine Hughes' efforts to rehabilitate herself and improve the quality of her life, and the lives of her children, can only be described as heroic. Francine was the daughter of parents who never completed grade school. Education was not highly valued, but Francine managed to stay in school until she was 16 years old. Her grades deteriorated as adolescence bloomed, but in grade school she had demonstrated abilities in math and English. Francine married Mickey Hughes when she was 16 and he was 18. She had her first child at 17 and three more children by the time she was 24.

Francine tried to work. She had a part-time waitress job for a few weeks in 1963 until Mickey took her out of the restaurant in the midst of the lunch hour rush. Sometime in the late 1960s, Francine worked in a nursing home for several weeks because Mickey had abandoned her and the children to go to Florida and there was nothing to eat. When Mickey returned from Florida, the job was over. Francine divorced Mickey in 1970 because it was the only way she could get Aid For Dependent Children. Mickey refused to support his family and had recently been fired from his job. Francine tried again in 1973 by working in a plastics factory. Mickey was now receiving Social Security Disability Insurance but none of this money was contributed to the family even though Mickey lived in the home Francine had purchased with her welfare income. Mickey's presence in the home was illegal, but Francine was advised that she would be the one prosecuted for welfare fraud, not Mickey. Mickey allowed Francine to work illegally so that they could purchase a car. When he took the family car away from her, she had no way to get to Lansing, Michigan, 20 miles from their home. Francine lost the job. In 1974, Francine obtained her General Equivalency Diploma (G.E.D.). She then worked part-time as a nurse's aide for seven months to prepare for entry into nursing school. Francine was now experiencing spells of dizziness and suffocation, which increased during her work as a nurse's aide. She quit the job. In 1976, she tried again. She applied for and received a Basic Opportunity Grant which paid for her tuition, books, and transportation at Lansing Business College. She started the secretarial course in September 1976. On March 9, 1977, Mickey Hughes burned Francine's books. Mickey Hughes died that night. Even in jail, awaiting trial, Francine persisted in her efforts to get an education. She completed her secretarial course by mail and enrolled in courses offered to inmates, including mathematics, American history, sociology, arts and crafts. Francine was acquitted in November 1977 and immediately went to work in a series of factory jobs. She was off welfare and supported herself and her children. In 1980, Francine Hughes enrolled in nursing school.

During all the years of their marriage, Mickey brutally beat Francine. He also expected sex upon demand and can be described as a marital rapist. He assaulted Francine verbally by calling her a "whore," a "slut," and "stupid." Toward the end, he was also violent toward his children and their pets (McNulty, 1980).

Francine's commitment to her own life, her own rehabilitation is reflected in the co-researchers' stories: *I wished I could have gone to Harvard–Sandra's Story; Now I'm working on my doctorate in human sexuality–Mary's Story; I'd like to go to law school–Grace's Story: I wanted to be a doctor–Liz's Story; I re-entered graduate school–Harriet's Story; I'd like to study sexism–Marlene's Story; Battered, battered, battered, and I decided to take this logic class–Anita's Story.*

Recognition of the efforts of abused women to save themselves and their children must also include a recognition of their efforts to vocationally rehabilitate themselves despite the odds against them. For Francine Hughes and the co-reseachers in this book, the development of a work identity is/was essential. As Harriet says: *My job saved my life.* Francine was able to save her own life only when her work identity was threatened.

The notion that women want to be on welfare, or that the newly divorced woman is lazy because she doesn't immediately go to work for minimum wages in the waged labor market, is proved false by the stories of Francine Hughes and the women in this book. For homemakers who experience rape, battering, and emotional abuse, the development of a work identity is almost impossible, if not a life-threatening activity. In the divorce process, women are now expected to either suddenly possess or quickly develop a usable work identity for the waged labor market. This is a highly stressful and confrontational process which is still poorly understood by career psychologists, attorneys, courts, and husbands. My recommendation to a family law attorney to give a formerly battered woman six months to do some pre-vocational work (e.g., recovery counseling and vocational exploration) prior to making vocational decisions was regarded as extreme, radical, and unusual. For women who work while being abused, the loss of an existing work identity is part of the abuse experience as we have seen in *Harriet's Story*. For some women abused as children, no work identity is allowed to surface at all, as we have seen in *Marlene's Story* and *Laura's Story*.

Recognition of the efforts of abused women to save themselves and their children must also include a recognition of their efforts to vocationally rehabilitate themselves despite the odds against them.

The loss of work identity in either the waged or unwaged work lives of women is a sort of death. When this loss occurs as the result of abuse, it is a kind of murder, soul murder (Miller, 1981, 1984a, 1984b, 1986, 1988). We have seen this in *Rhonda's, Laura's, Marlene's,* and *Liz's Stories*. For these women, either the life of work is lost altogether or reduced to work far below the skill level possessed before the abuse. In summary, some women don't make it through. This is why I have proposed a life care plan for Laura and Marlene rather than a vocational rehabilitation plan. In my opinion, the loss of work identity development as well as the loss of entire professions as a result of abuse falls into the category of hedonic damages.

I chose the story of Francine Hughes to demonstrate how the attempted destruction of her work identity is a kind of wrongful death, and because there is a wrongful death–Mickey Hughes' death. Therefore, the lost earning capacity analysis developed here will include an analysis for both Mickey and Francine Hughes. I include Francine because this death could have been her death, and because doing both analyses allows for a comparison between Mickey and Francine in terms of their respective financial contributions to their children, themselves, and each other.

Presenting an analysis for hedonic damages is highly problematic since data used by economists to testify as to the value of hedonic damages do not appear to be available for domestic violence cases. For example, "in product liability cases, the amount spent on life saving can be compared to societal norms. It may be that a $.25 part can save one life for every 10 million products sold, implying that the manufacturer values life at $2.5 million" (Smith, 1988, p. 70). What is the equivalent here? The cost of supporting shelter services for battered women and their children per life lost? The cost of implementing laws such as Oregon's Mandatory Arrest Statutes which might have saved Mickey Hughes' life if such a law existed in Michigan at the time of his death? Under a mandatory arrest statute, Mickey Hughes would have been automatically arrested every time he beat up Francine (Woods, 1981). A study conducted in Minneapolis indicated that mandatory arrest might be the most effective approach in preventing further abuse (Woods, 1981). Such an analysis is beyond the scope of this book. Therefore, hedonic damages will be set within the range previously awarded–$500,000 to $3.5 million, or at Magrowski's (1991) range of $27,095 to $209,917.

Adding to the complexity of evaluating hedonic damages is the fact that few courts have addressed the issue of whether one spouse can sue another in a wrongful death case (Karp & Karp, 1989). However, most states do allow an action for any wrongful act, neglect, or default that causes death (Karp & Karp, 1989). Such suits have been filed against police departments for denying battered women legal protection (Gundle, 1986). In civil sexual assault cases, hedonic damages are awarded to spouses for loss of consortium (sexual pleasure) (Institute for the Study of Sexual Assault, 1983-1987). Wrongful death suits are also being filed in civil sexual assault cases (Institute for the Study of Sexual Assault, 1983- 1987). Again, it is not the job of the vocational expert to determine against whom such cases should be filed but to provide information to attorneys, judges, and/or juries.

The trial date is arbitrarily chosen for September 9, 1978. Francine's birthdate is unknown, but is set at August 1, 1947. Her date of "death" is set at the date of Mickey Hughes' actual death which is March 9, 1977. Francine is white and her worklife expectancy at the time of the trial was 22.6 years (Fredlund, 1986-1989).

Hypothetical #1: If Francine Hughes had not "died" on 3/9/77, she would have completed her secretarial course at the Lansing Business College and gone to work as a secretary by 9/30/77 for a starting salary and a 15% benefit ratio equivalent to $5,461 yearly (United States Department of Labor, Bureau of Labor Statistics, 1977-1978). Her lost earnings over her worklife expectancy would have been $127,704. With adjustment for the discount rate, the damage award to her children would have been between **$83,923** and **$102,579**.

Hypothetical #2: If Francine Hughes had not "died" on 3/9/77, what would have been the value of her household services less consumption? Consumption is defined as the money a person uses to care for him- or herself (e.g., haircuts, medical expenses, clothes, food, toiletries). An average consumption rate for a parent with three children at home is 17.2% of the value of household services (Metcalf, 1990a). If the value of household services is set at the minimum wage in 1971 ($1.60 per hour) and Francine worked 55 hours per week in the home, then the value of her household services less 17.2% consumption is **$52,997** (Field, 1989).

Hypothetical #3: The value of Francine Hughes' life is greater than her lost earning capacity as a secretary and provider of household services. The hedonic damages have a wide range of possibilities as noted above. If Francine Hughes had died on March 9, 1977, the value of her household services would be considered greater than the value of her waged work as a secretary by her children because part of her household services was to protect them from their father's violence.

> *I am led to the conviction that mandatory arrest and treatment programs for batterers may give them the only chance they have to make a valuable life.*

Mickey Hughes was a high school drop-out and an alcoholic. He had a short work history which started in 1962 and ended in 1970 as a result of a serious automobile accident. Mickey had a series of jobs as a construction worker and factory worker. He did become a skilled worker as a brick mason or brick layer earning $8.00 per hour at his highest earning level, but was unable to keep a job longer than a few weeks or months. He was also considered to be a skilled mechanic. He received Social Security Disability Insurance (SSDI) after his accident, from 1970 until the day of his death. This income was equivalent to the income Francine received from Aid For Dependent Children (AFDC), but he did not contribute any of this income to his family, using it all for himself (McNulty, 1980). SSDI and AFDC income are considered collateral income and cannot be presented to juries in personal injury or wrongful death cases (Minzer, Nates, Kimball, & Goldstein, 1989).

The trial date is set at September 8, 1978. Mickey's birthday is in 1945 with January 1 chosen as his date of birth. His date of death is March 9, 1977. His worklife expectancy from that date would be 27.3 years (The shorter worklife expectancies of women is revealed here with Francine's at 22.6 years. Women's discontinuous work lives are reflected in these statistics.) (Fredlund, 1986-1989).

Hypothetical #1: If Mickey Hughes had lived and been able to overcome the disability caused by his automobile accident, what would his lost earning capacity have been? The assumptions are that he would have been unable to return to his highest paying job of brick layer due to his disability. He would have had to return to factory work at $4.25 per hour as his highest wage. He would have had overcome his alcoholism and maintained a stable work pattern. The last two assumptions are, of course, highly unlikely. Mickey Hughes' work history was erratic, and at the time of his death he was on disability income. However, in an optimistic posture, we will assume that he settled down into 29.1 years of stable work with wages and benefits starting at $10,086. His earnings would have been $287,510. Adjustment for the discount rate would have put the damage award to his children at between **$200,901** to **237,624.**

Hypothetical #2: Since Mickey Hughes provided no household services whatsoever, there is no loss of household services. The issue of consumption is interesting because Mickey Hughes used all of his disability income for himself, not sharing any of it with his wife or his children. In addition, he illegally consumed a portion of his wife's and children's AFDC income as well.

Hypothetical #3: The value of Mickey Hughes' life is greater than his lost earning capacity. What is the hedonic value of Mickey Hughes' life? This is a difficult question since Mickey Hughes had no consistent work history and no apparent intentions of creating one. So using a work history or possible lost earnings on which to base a hedonic award appears unlikely. Since Mickey's consumption appears to outweigh his contribution to his family, a basis for hedonic value cannot be located there either. In comparison, I am not prepared to state that Mickey Hughes' life had no value at all. In pondering the value of his life, I am led to the conviction that mandatory arrest and treatment programs for batterers may give them the only chance they have to make a valuable life. Therefore, the hedonic value of Mickey Hughes' life, in my opinion, is that it was a life worth trying to save.

I feel so tremendously proud.

–from *Anita's Story*

anita's story*

    I'm 32 years old and I'm from San Diego. I have a twin sister who lives in Washington, D.C. My parents separated when I was 12 years old. Actually, I was raised in Chula Vista, right across the border from Tijuana. I'm bilingual and I was raised with strong ties to my grandparents and extended family living in Mexico. I was very close to my grandmother. She was a battered woman, too. My mother was, and still is, a battered woman. My father physically abused her, and she is verbally abused by her present husband. My father, my grandfather, and my mother all drank, but I think my mother drank while she was being battered by my father.

    Both my twin and I were spanked by my father. It was not the kind of spanking to discipline. There wasn't time out to talk. There was a feeling of a loss of control. I can still feel the anger from his spirit, from his soul. That's still clear, very clear. My twin and I had each other until we were 14 when my grandmother died. We were good little girls who didn't make too much noise. Can you see our starched dresses? Those horrible petticoats! And our hair having to be all swooped up, and out of our faces. Every strand perfect. My father was such a perfectionist.

    There's a lot of pain here. I feel shamed. My twin and I used to fight each other, hurt each other. We've talked about it. There is some healing. Neither of us have ever married. She's lived with her partner for five years. It was a holding onto my soul, to not get married. It was the last thing I held out on with my batterer. "No. You don't have papers on me." My sister's like that, too. We've talked about it.

    Our parents divorced and my sister moved away with my mother and I stayed with my grandfather. I lost my parents, my twin, and my grandmother all at once. I became the woman of the house. I cooked

---

*In her own words.

every night, but my grandfather did do the laundry. When I was 16, I went to work as a store clerk. I met my batterer there. He worked next door at the gas station. He was 20. He had a big black beard, long hair. He was witty, a good sense of humor, very macho. We started dating. I was dating other guys, and later, I found out he was living with another woman while he was dating me. He was very possessive. He would roar by on his motorcycle when I was with someone else at my house. It was as though he were saying, "I'm watching you." That started right away. I finished high school, but it was hard. I felt lonely and I felt overloaded with responsibility from home and school. I wanted to move out with Richard and go to college. My grandfather didn't want me to leave so he said, "Why don't you both just live with me?" So we did, for about a year. I thought, "I'll tame this stallion. I'll fix him. I'll change him." I had those feelings from the beginning.

I started college. He wanted to know my schedule, my itinerary. He didn't encourage me to go to school, but he didn't discourage me. I encouraged him. Then he went to the university and he would drive my car, drop me off and pick me up. He had control over the transportation. He went to the university and I went to the community college. He is Anglo, and I think I had internalized racism. I didn't think I was good enough to go to the university. I had to go to community college. The pushing started then, I think. It's not very clear to me. He'd say, "Don't be a baby. Don't be a wimp." We were still living with my grandfather.

Then we moved into a nice two-bedroom apartment with a gym and a pool. We could afford our own apartment because we were both working and going to school. The violence escalated. No black eyes, but bruises on hidden parts of my body. I used to wonder if the two old ladies downstairs could hear all the noise. I didn't want to wake them up. I worked in a hospital as a ward clerk. I was also interpreting, of course, for patients. No extra money for that, though. Some days I just went to work, headed for the bathroom, and cried. There I am in a hospital, and I didn't feel safe enough to tell a nurse. I sensed that people at work knew something was wrong. I came to work on the back of Rick's motorcycle when the car wasn't working, and I remember how the nurses scolded me for not wearing a helmet. But I didn't care. I was very unhappy. I didn't value my life. I worked 20 to 30 hours per week. I know I was underpaid. I took two or three classes at a time. It was a real strain for me at work. Then I dropped out of my anatomy class. I just couldn't concentrate. I couldn't study at home. "You're taking too much time on studying. You're not spending time with me." There was battering during studying. And so it went. I'd go to school, and he'd follow me. Then I would drop out or he would drop out but it was always him following me, keeping track of me. My last class in college was logic. Battered, battered, battered, and I decided to take this logic class. I decided I was going to prove to him that I was smart. I always work hard in school. I have to study a lot. I worked my butt off. I went to a study group. I didn't flunk. I got a "D." It was an achievement. I did my best.

I got pregnant. I told him I was going to get an abortion. I didn't ask him, I told him. I still, for the life of me, don't believe I was able to do this. The abuse escalated after that. One time I was running out of the apartment building toward the parking lot. He grabbed me. He was about six feet and weighed 180 or 190 pounds. I was around 105. He dragged me by my hair up the stairs into the stairwell. I remember wondering: "Is anybody looking at this?" I felt shame.

After that I left him. My father helped me, but he said, "I'm going to help you get out this time, but I won't do it again." He helped me pack up and I moved to San Jose where my mother lived with her new husband. Somehow, Rick thought I had gone to Washington, D.C. where my sister was. He drove there looking for me, and back across the country again. I was scared to death, looking over my shoulder. I never talked to anyone about it. I never connected it to being battered. I had lived with him for two years.

I stayed away from him for a year. I got a job as a secretary, and I had my own apartment in San Jose. The job was boring, horrible. Eight hours every day being in an office. I was lonely and bored, and along came Rick. He called me up. He had moved to Santa Cruz. Within two or three months, I was living with him again. I gave up my full-time job and I went with him.

I had a new car and a new car payment, but it was all going to be hunky dory because we were going to live by the ocean. Everything was going to be fine.

We did drugs, mostly speed, black beauties. I got afraid of using them, feeling out of control. I just stopped. Stopped for awhile. I could back off from it. We both drank and he did the drugs and the alcohol to smooth it out. I guess the battering started right away. I'm very blocked on it. It was very severe but I can't remember. I got a job as a mail clerk. Low paying, horrid job. No, not at the post office. Don't I wish! Rick is making 10 or 15 dollars per hour as a mechanic, and I'm making maybe five or six dollars, if that. Then I got a job at a hotel in personnel. I really liked it. I got good feedback from the Latino community. I was helping with hiring and explaining company policy to the new employees. I had to use my Spanish. I was going to write a newsletter, but it ended up in the hands of an Anglo woman with a college degree. She was supportive of me and all that, but somehow, that employee newsletter got taken away from me. Then there were layoffs, and I was told I could take a job in the accounting department or have no job at all. So I went back to school to take accounting. I'm still being battered.

Then it started again. "School is taking time away from us. You're too stupid anyway. Dumb Mexican." Battering during studying. He got a big job in Santa Clara. He expected me to relocate with him, to work with him. Now we drove into work together. He was the service manager for this big dealership making about $500 per week. And, oh, this makes me so angry! I was making maybe $250, while he's out of the office. I'm doing the same job he's doing, but he's getting double the money. This went on for two or three years until he had a work accident. He was drunk at the time. Drinking, drug use, physical and sexual violence. I started Al-Anon. The battering got worse when I was under his complete control–at home and at work. I was afraid he was going to kill someone when he drove. He was drinking about a quart of whiskey per day after the accident. I was so afraid. The owner of the dealership wanted me to keep working, but I felt it would be a betrayal of Rick, and so I didn't work for over a year. It was the bottom.

Then some episode happened. I don't remember what it was. I didn't care anymore. I didn't care what he did to me. I didn't care if he killed me. Do it. By then, I knew I had done everything I could. He put his hands around my neck, ...and that feeling of being choked. I wasn't going to take it anymore. I left that day, and that was five years ago.

I went to a friend's home, a friend I had made in Al-Anon. We didn't talk directly about battering in Al-Anon. Nobody had to use the word but I think they knew. They said, "You don't deserve to be a doormat. You don't deserve this. You don't deserve that." I went to a conference once where they did address physical violence but, in this case, they stayed together. He was a nice recovering alcoholic. And I said to myself, "Why in her story did it turn out so nice? Why did I get cheated?" People said I was co-dependent. I was able to understand some of it, but it didn't work. I would walk out of the room. Then I'm locking myself into a room. Then why is he breaking down the door? Why isn't this Al-Anon stuff working? The day I left he stole my car. I filed a report, but I didn't get my car back for months. So, here I am trying to look for a job without a car. It just makes me so angry. He had all the money. Seventy-five thousand in the bank, stocks. All gone, money we had accumulated. In all those years of abuse, I called the police just once. They did not separate us. Rick gave me one of those power glares of his as if to say, "You keep your mouth shut, Bitch!" Here are these two men in uniform. I'm going to trust them?

After I left, I got into therapy with probably the best therapist for domestic violence around. I'm really grateful to her. She had sensitivity to battered women and was a leader to me, and all the women in my group. We were a cohesive support for each other to not go back. They were my lifeline to stay away from him, and then I got pregnant by another man and had a child. I planned it because I knew I wouldn't go back to Rick if I had a child. My child was my salvation.

One of the dreams I had before I left was of a bird flying up. I was flying up, up, up. I was breaking away. It was very sad but there was so much relief at the breaking of the chains. At the very end, I had started to keep a journal. I kept it at work. I wrote, ''I must leave or die.'' I read it over and over. Journal work is so important for battered women, for everybody.

He was very much into bondage. He made me go with him to a porno film once, and he also had a box of porno magazines. In my survivor's group we didn't tap into the sexual abuse. It's so deep and internalized, still. I hated it. Hated the hurt. It's scary stuff because it's so intimate. These are the things your partner, whom you loved, did to you. Feeling like a prostitute, feeling used, feeling degraded, feeling humiliated. It's still not talked about, even within the battered women's movement.

I went back to work six months after leaving him. I lived on money my mother gave back to me after I had loaned it to her. I couldn't really work. I was going to therapy, my support group, and Al-Anon, too. I tried to get help from welfare. That was a joke. They wouldn't help me because I wasn't homeless. I went to the State Department of Rehabilitation. I told them that I had been battered for years, and that I needed to get into some sort of program. They did a one- or two-hour intake and that was it. They didn't see any bruises on me, no marks. Nothing was done. I never heard back from them. I went to an attorney but it was just a joke—the lack of protection for battered women who have been coerced to sign whatever, to sign their homes over to their partners. I decided that if Rick had the filthy money, then maybe he'd leave me alone. I guess I bought my way out.

I went back to work as a secretary and then I saw a job opening at a shelter. I had doubts. Am I ready? I didn't have a college degree but I did have personal experience. I got the job. I had lots of support from other survivors. I wouldn't have been able to do it without their support. It was hard. I was still not in control of any of my flashbacks, and there I was. I'm speaking in a woman's group, and it's all white. I'm representing the agency. I'm trying to stay in control, and all of the sudden, I see a woman on the ground with a sheet over her. A powerful vision and all this sadness coming into me. ''Anita, you're at a luncheon. Hold yourself together.'' I didn't feel safe until

I got back to the shelter. Then I broke down. I hadn't felt safe to cry at the luncheon.

I worked at the shelter for more than a year. I got power, more power to myself. Giving myself power, power, power. Feeling stronger. A court advocate job came up, a court advocate position for a domestic violence coordinator. There was a supervisory position and an advocate position. I decided to go for the advocate job. My friends said, "No. Go for the supervisor job, Anita." I'm working for the City Attorney's office! I'm the supervisor. I've been there two months. I'm making much more than at the shelter. Shelter workers are not acknowledged for their work, you know. They do a hell of a job. In this job I make around $2,000 per month and I've got benefits. There is job mobility. I can get raises.

I feel so tremendously proud.

eleven

---

a feminist vocational rehabilitation model

It has been the accepted wisdom that emotional problems are central causes of psychopathology and that only by alleviating emotional difficulties can intellectual deficits be ameliorated. Our stories and the works of Reuven Feuerstein (1980), Nicholas Hobbs (1982), and Myrna Shure and George Spivack (1978) all suggest the central importance of intellectual development if emotional difficulties are to be prevented or overcome. "Gaining a voice" and developing an awareness of their own minds are the tasks that these women must accomplish if they are to cease being either a perpetrator or a victim of family violence."
(Belenky, Clinchy, Goldberger, & Tarule, 1986, p. 163)

The Three Laws of Recovery: Law #1: Sobriety is the first priority. Law #2: Trust your hesitations. Law #3: You decide. (Neland, undated)

What matters is that lives do not serve as models; only stories do that. And it is a hard thing to make up stories to live by. We can only retell and live by the stories we have heard or read. We live our lives through texts. They may be read, or chanted, or experienced electronically, or come to us, like the murmurings of our mothers, telling us what conventions demand. Whatever their form or medium, these stories have formed us all; they are what we must use to make new fictions, new narratives. (Heilbrun, 1988, p. 37)

This book has been about stories: the co-researcher's stories, Francine Hughes' story, my stories of vocational rehabilitation practice with abused women, stories based on cases in rehabilitation and in the courts. A feminist vocational rehabilitation model is just another story formed out of the stories which have gone before. Out of these stories comes a new narrative, a new story to be used in vocational rehabilitation practice, in the courts, and a new story to live by.

A feminist vocational rehabilitation model is women-centered. That is, it is based on the lives of women. (The word *women* here does not refer to *white women* but refers to *women* with the recognition of the irreducible experiences of class, ethnicity, age, abuse trauma[s]). This means the acknowledgment of and the advocacy for the right of women to develop, possess, and nurture a work identity. This means acknowledgment of women as workers in the waged labor market and in the unwaged work of caring for children, elders, and the disabled. This means knowing women working in the home contribute 55 hours per week to homemaking activities, and women working in the waged labor market and in the home contribute 22 hours per week to homemaking activities; in contrast to husbands who contribute eleven hours or less to homemaking services (Field, 1989). This means knowing that women's work patterns differ from male work patterns, but also knowing that this does not diminish them as workers. A woman's worklife is a complex mosaic of her choices (if she has choices); her access to education, transportation, and occupations; and her family responsibilities. This means knowing that women earn less money than men no matter what they do, but also knowing that this is a reflection of the systematic economic oppression of women, and is no reflection on the skills, desires, aspirations, achievements, and contributions of women as workers in both waged and unwaged work. In this model, a woman's social role as wife and mother is never allowed to erase her role as a worker in either waged or unwaged work.

A feminist vocational rehabilitation model is women-centered. That is, based on the reality of the pervasive violence which permeates so many women's lives. This means acknowledgment of the traumatic and profound distortions which violence introduces into every woman's efforts to develop, possess, and nurture a work identity in the waged and unwaged work worlds. The feminist vocational rehabilitation model acknowledges prostituted women as abused women, and includes all abused women (abused disabled women, dominant culture women, women of color, women of all classes and ethnicity) within the call for advocacy.

The feminist vocational rehabilitation model is women-centered. That is, based on the reality of injury to women who have experienced abuse. These injuries are both psychological and physical. The feminist rehabilitationist is well-versed in the post-traumatic stress disorder syndrome and in its subcategories: Rape Trauma Syndrome, Battered Women Syndrome, and Child Abuse Accommodation Syndrome. The feminist rehabilitationist understands the minimizing and denial process, by both survivors and society at large, which functions to make physical injuries to abuse survivors invisible or inconsequential. The pervasive nature of psychological and physical injuries requires the taking of an abuse history along with a vocational history at the time of the initial meeting between the client and the rehabilitationist. The feminist rehabilitationist knows that the years when vocational identity formation generally occurs are also the years when a woman is statistically the most vulnerable to being raped; including marital rape and extortion or inducement into prostitution. Therefore, careful attention is paid to these years (13 to 26) in a woman's life no matter what her age is at the time of the initial meeting.

The model also contains a protocol for working with survivors so that the safety of both the survivor and the rehabilitationist and any other parties to the process (e.g., clerical staff, other professionals, shelter workers) is insured. Possible injury from batterers, pimps, perpetrators of incest and battery are acknowledged as real and not ignored. This protocol is written and available to all staff who may be working with the survivor. Perpetrators may exhibit the following behaviors:

> Over-solicitous attention to the client should arouse suspicion. Someone with information to hide will try to stay with the victim to prevent her from making accusations or seeking help. Batterers, rapists, and pimps have been known to bully their way into interviewing offices, often intimidating personnel. At other times, perpetrators take a very compliant, remorseful posture, hoping to engender the sympathy of the staff. Or they may impersonate family members or authorities (e.g., police officers, security guards, probation officers) on the telephone to obtain information about the victim. They may threaten children of the victim (Arnett, 1990).

A suggested protocol (Arnett, 1990) includes:

1. The maintenance of confidentiality. No information is given to unauthorized persons for any reason. NEVER REVEAL THE LOCATION OF A SHELTER OR SAFE HOUSE.
2. Call police or security to have perpetrators removed if the perpetrator does not respond to calm and firm requests to leave the premises.
3. Report threats to children to the appropriate authorities.
4. Arrange for private and quiet space to meet with the client. Survivors are unlikely to speak frankly if children, the perpetrator, or others are present.
5. Inform the client of her rights to privacy and confidentiality.
6. Do not rush in to save the client, pressure her to file a complaint, or demand that she get a divorce or leave her pimp.
7. Develop trust, rapport, and respect between you and the client.
8. Assist the client with arrangements for escape after the meeting, if needed.
9. Assist the client with a plan of action (lists of resources, support systems) for herself (and children, if needed) if she chooses to return to the abusive environment.

10. Provide the client with factual information on abuse
     dynamics (e.g., Walker's Cycle of Violence).

*The feminist vocational rehabilitation model is women-
centered.* That is, based on a respect for women's abilities to
manage their own recoveries. Coercion, even in the name
of a women's best interest, is not within this model. A
woman who returns to her battering husband or pimp is
grieved, but not denigrated or reported to the police. She is
always welcome to return as she tries and tries again. The
role of the rehabilitationist, in the feminist model, is to
provide information, support, resources, and advocacy as
the woman follows the three laws of recovery outlined by
Neland (undated) in the opening of this chapter.
Rehabilitationists working with survivors inside such systems as workers' compensation and state departments of
rehabilitation make every effort to explain the constraints
and restrictions of these systems to survivors so that loss of
benefits to the survivors do not take place or are not minimized. Part of the advocacy for survivors in such systems is
to help the survivors understand that their possible inability
to use such systems is not their fault. Survivors will then be
directed to other resources.

---

*Coercion, even in the name
of a women's best interest, is
not within this model.*

---

*The feminist vocational rehabilitation model is women-
centered.* That is, based on the achievements of women in
opening the many paths to recovery we see reflected in this
book. These paths include: 12-Step programs such as AA,
NA, AL-ANON, ACA groups; re-birthing, massage, and
other body work techniques; co-dependency groups; journal work; incest, rape, battering, and prostitution recovery
work in individual therapy and group processes; volunteer
and staff work with rape crisis centers, prostitution recovery
services, and battered women's shelter services; women's

studies classes; the hearing and telling of abuse stories through books, films, consciousness raising groups, and counseling sessions.

The feminist vocational rehabilitation model is women-centered. That is, based on an ethic that intellectual development is important for abused women since part of their abuse has been verbal-emotional (Theodoulou, 1990) and centered upon their supposed lack of competencies and intellectual abilities.

> A woman, like any other human being, does need to know that the mind makes mistakes; but our interviews have convinced us that every woman, regardless of age, social class, ethnicity, and academic achievement, needs to know that she is capable of intelligent thought, and she needs to know it right away. (Belenky, Clinchy, Goldberger, & Tarule, 1986, p. 193)

This understanding allows the feminist rehabilitationist to assist the survivor in selecting training programs suited to her needs. For some survivors, pre-vocational work may be necessary prior to the survivor's choice of a vocational goal. This may include: recovery work (battered women groups, rape crisis counseling), literacy training, study skill development, remedial math and English courses, desensitization to overcome fear of academic settings, hands-on skill training, parenting classes, and extensive vocational exploration (e.g., aptitude and interest testing, informational interviews, job trials).

...intellectual development is important for abused women since part of their abuse has been verbal-emotional (Theodoulou, 1990) and centered upon their supposed lack of competencies and intellectual abilities.

The feminist vocational rehabilitation model is women-centered. That is, based upon an understanding of the complexity of women's lives. This means the development of vocational rehabilitation plans which incorporate all of the elements described above: development of work identity, acknowledgment of women's unwaged work lives, acknowledgment of psychological and physical injuries which may result in vocational impairment, respect and support for the survivor's recovery process, and advocacy for the survivor's need for intellectual and skill development as part of her recovery process. The model also draws upon the standards and ethics developed by the rehabilitation profession (see Appendix 4), in providing services while incorporating the special needs of abuse survivors into the provision of services.

Feminist rehabilitationists also understand how their own abuse histories may impede their ability to provide services. Consequently, they will undertake their own recovery process in order to provide the best quality of service in casework rehabilitation systems, in rape crisis, battered women, and prostitution recovery settings, or in vocational expert witness testimony in the courts.

Feminist rehabilitationists also understand how their own abuse histories may impede their ability to provide services.

Rehabilitationists serving survivors as vocational experts will draw upon the 25 areas of required expertise described in Chapter Six and summarized into Appendix 5.

And finally, the model includes an advocacy role on a political/social level. This advocacy was implemented at the National Conference of the National Coalition Against Domestic Violence (NCADV) on August 4, 1990 by the NCADV in their Annual Membership Meeting held at the University of Massachusetts at Amherst. The Resolution was adopted by the NCADV and represents an effort to bring together concerned private sector rehabilitationists with abuse survivors in the Making the Connections Project. The Resolution is reprinted in Appendix 6.

This resolution is obviously a beginning because it does not address the concerns of rape, incest, or prostitution survivors. It does not suggest a method by which abuse survivors can gain access to proper medical evaluation and treatment. However, it does provide the yeast which will allow feminist rehabilitationists and/or knowledgeable survivors (some of us are both) to rise up together in creating a whole loaf for the women survivors of abuse. Crumbs will no longer do. We are not beggars at the feast of life, or to put it hedonically, we deserve the whole loaf (Waring, 1988). After all, as Chicago (1979) would point out in her magnificently illustrated story, *The Dinner Party: A Symbol of Our Heritage*, we deserve the whole loaf because we baked it.

references

American Psychiatric Association. (1987). *Diagnostic and statistical manual of mental disorders* (3rd ed., rev.). Washington, DC: Author.

Americans with Disabilities Act of 1990. P.L. 101-336.

Amott, T. L., & Matthaei, J. A. (1991). *Race, gender & work: A multicultural history of women in the United States* (pp. 11-30). Boston: South End Press.

Anderson, A. F., & McMaken, M. E. (1990). Implementing child advocacy: A rational and basic blueprint. *Juvenile & Family Court Journal, 41*, 1-14.

Anderson, B., Frank, E., & Moss, M. (1991, February). Empirical status of rape trauma. *Violence Update*, p. 1.

Armstrong, L. (1978). *Kiss daddy goodnight: A speak-out on incest.* New York: Pocket Books.

Armstrong, L. (1990). The personal is apolitical. *The Women's Review of Books, VII*, 1-3.

Arnett, C. (1990). *A domestic violence protocol for rehabilitationists.* Unpublished manuscript.

Baldwin, M. (Speaker). (1990, July). *Prostitution and rape law* (Cassette Recording). Washington, DC: National Coalition Against Sexual Assault.

Barry, K. (1979). *Female sexual slavery.* New York: New York University Press.

Barry, K. (1991, January) Profile. *Violence Update*, p. 4.

Bateson, M. C. (1991, February). *Creative couples and gender complementarity: Cross-disciplinary perspectives.* Symposium conducted at the meeting of the American Academy For the Advancement of Science, Washington D.C.

Belenky, M. F., Clinchy, B. M., Goldberger, N. R., & Tarule, J. M. (1986). *Women's ways of knowing: The development of self, voice, and mind.* New York: Basic Books.

Bell, C. (1991, January 20). Women and homicides. *Parade Magazine*, p. 17.

Bell, L. (Ed.). (1987). From the floor. In L. Bell (Ed.), *Good girls, bad girls: Feminists and sex trade workers face to face.* (pp. 114-115). Seattle: The Seal Press.

Berkowitz, M., & Greene, C. (1989, Spring). Disability expenditures. *American Rehabilitation*, pp. 7-29.

Berube, A. (1990). *Coming out under fire: The history of gay men and women in World War Two.* New York: The Free Press.

Boland, M. L. (1990a). *Expert testimony in sexual abuse/sexual assault: Selected cases.* Unpublished manuscript.

Boland, M. L. (1990b). *Psychological evidence: Criminal sexual assault/abuse.* Unpublished manuscript.

Bornn, N. (1990). Sexual harassment update. In P. R. Herson (Ed.), *Current issues in employment law* (pp. 1-16). Berkeley: CEB Publications.

Bowen, N. H. (1982, December). Counseling with abused women. *The Vocational Guidance Quarterly, 65*, 123-127.

Brandi, D. (1990). Education for our lives: Women redefining global economic development. *NWSAction*, Fall, p. 8.

Browne, A. (1987). *When battered women kill.* New York: The Free Press.

Brownmiller, S. (1975). *Against our will: Men, women & rape.* New York: Simon & Schuster.

Bruyere, S. (1986). An existentialist approach to rehabilitation counseling. In T. E. Backer (Ed.), *Applied rehabilitation counseling* (pp. 125-134). New York: Springer Publishing Company.

Burgess, A. W. & Holmstrom, L. L. (1985). Rape trauma syndrome and post traumatic stress response. In A. W. Burgess (Ed.), *Rape and sexual assault* (pp. 46-60). New York: Garland Publishing.

California Civil Code 4801 (a)-(f), Standard California Codes (1992 Ed.). New York: Matthew Bender.

California Federation BPW/USA proposed 1990-1991 legislative platform. (1990, July, August, September). *California Woman*, p. 32.

California Workers' Compensation Institute (1990, June). *Research notes: Mental stress claims.* San Francisco: Author.

California Workers' Compensation Institute (1990, November). *The incidence of disabling work injuries and illnesses in California dropped last year* (Bulletin No. 90-20). San Francisco: Author.

Campagna, D. S., & Poffenberger, D. L. (1988). *Sexual trafficking in children.* Dover, MA: Auburn House Publishing Company.

Campbell, J. C. (1990, December). Battered woman syndrome: A critical review. *Violence Update*, p. 4.

Capitol update. (1991, Winter). *National Business Woman*, p. 5.

Caputi, J. (1987). *The age of sex crime.* Bowling Green, OH: Bowling Green State University Press.

CBS News. (1991, January 27). *60 minutes*, vol. XXIII (20).

Chicago, J. (1979). *The dinner party: A symbol of our heritage.* Garden City, NY: Anchor Books.

Connors, D. (1985). Disability, sexism and the social order. In S. E. Browne, D. Connors, & N. Stern (Eds.), *With the power of each breath: A disabled woman's anthology* (pp. 92-107). Pittsburgh: Cleis Press.

Continuing Education of the Bar. (1990, April). *Current issues in employment law: Program handbook.* Berkeley: Author.

Coudroglou, A., & Poole, D. L. (1984). *Disability, work & social policy.* New York: Springer Publishing Company.

Daniele, Y. (1985). The treatment and prevention of long-term effects and intergenerational transmission of victimization: A lesson from holocaust survivors and their children. In C. R. Figley (Ed.), *Trauma and its wake: The study and treatment of post-traumatic stress disorder* (pp. 295-313). New York: Brunner/Mazel.

Deane, N. (1990, Spring). Issue specialist report: Equal educational opportunity. *National Business Woman*, pp. 30, 32.

Deneen, L. J. (1991, January). Reemployment: Displaced vs. disabled. *CARP Newsletter*, p. 1.

Despres, P. F. C. (1990, Fall). Letters from readers. *Headlines: The Brain Injury Magazine*, p. 17.

Deutsch, P. M. (1985). *Rehabilitation testimony: Maintaining a professional perspective.* New York: Matthew Bender.

Deutsch, P. M., & Fralish, K. B. (1990). *Innovations in head injury rehabilitation.* New York: Matthew Bender.

Deutsch, P. M., & Sawyer, H. W. (1989). *A guide to rehabilitation.* New York: Matthew Bender.

Domingo, C. (Ed.) (1990, November). *Clearinghouse On Femicide Newsletter*, p. 1.

Donaldson, M. A., & Gardner, R. (1985). Diagnosis and treatment of traumatic stress among women after childhood incest. In C. R. Figley (Ed.), *Trauma and its wake: The study and treatment of post-traumatic stress disorder* (pp. 356-377). New York: Brunner/Mazel.

Donovan, L. A. (1987). For a paralyzed woman raped and murdered while alone in her own apartment. In M. Simon & F. Howe (Eds.), *With wings: An anthology of literature by and about women with disabilities* (pp. 31-32). New York: The Feminist Press.

Doweiko, H. E. (1990). *Concepts of chemical dependency.* Pacific Grove, CA: Brooks/Cole Publishing.

Dworkin, A. (1989). *Letters from a war zone: Writings 1976-1989.* New York: E. F. Dutton.

Dworkin, A. (1976). *Our blood: Prophecies and discourses on sexual politics.* New York: Harper & Row.

Dworkin, A., & MacKinnon, C. A. (1988). *Pornography & civil rights: A new day for women's equality.* Minneapolis: Organizing Against Pornography.

Edwards, H. (1990, March). A Canadian sunset: A litany for fourteen murdered women. *Off Our Backs*, p. 26.

Ehrlich, S. (1989). *Lisa, Hedda, & Joel: The Steinberg murder case*. New York: St. Martin's Press.

Enloe, C. (1989). *Bananas, beaches & bases: Making feminist sense of international politics*. Berkeley: University of California Press.

Fanning, J. (1990, Spring). What are the options? *Headlines: The Brain Injury Magazine*, p. 10.

Fearn, C. F. (1990, July). New legislation may change California's GAIN program. *Economic Justice Speakout, 4*, 21-22.

Field, T. F. (Ed.). (1989). The value and worth of housewives and household activities. *The Professional Reader, 1*, 1.

Field, T. F. (1990, November). Developing a case: Formulating your opinion. *The Field Report, 5*, 1-6.

Field, T. G., & Field, J. E. (1990). *Estimating a person's employability and wage earning capacity: Using the new QUEST program*. Athens, GA: Elliott & Fitzpatrick.

Figley, C. R. (Ed.). (1985). *Trauma and its wake: The study and treatment of posttraumatic stress disorder*. New York: Brunner/Mazel.

Finkelhor, D., Gelles, R. J., Hotaling, G. T., & Straus, M. A. (Eds.). (1983). *The dark side of families: Current family violence research*. Beverly Hills: Sage Publications.

Finkelhor, D., & Yllo, K. (1985). *License to rape: Sexual abuse of wives*. New York: Holt, Rinehart and Winston.

Fitzgerald, L. F., & Crites, J. O. (1980). Toward a career psychology of women: What do we know? What do we need to know? *Journal of Counseling Psychology, 27*(1), 4-62.

Fredlund, M. C. (1986-1989). *Personal injury economist* (Computer program). Oakland, CA: Advocate Software, Inc.

Freud, S. (1966). *The complete introductory lectures of psychoanalysis*. New York: Norton.

Gelles, R. J., & Straus, M. A. (1988). *Intimate violence: The causes and consequences of abuse in the American family*. New York: Touchstone.

Gerstel, N., & Gross, H. E. (1987). Introduction and overview. In N. Gerstel & H. E. Gross (Eds.), *Families and work* (pp. 4-7). Philadelphia: Temple University Press.

Giobbe, E. (1990). *A facilitator's guide to prostitution: A matter of violence against women*. Minneapolis: WHISPER, Inc.

Glazer, N. (1987). Servants to capital: Unpaid domestic labor and paid work. In N. Gerstel & H. E. Gross (Eds.), *Families and work* (pp. 236-255). Philadelphia: Temple University Press.

Goldman, E. (1970). *The traffic in women and other essays on feminism*. Albion, CA: Times Change Press.

Goleman, D. (1990, June 12). Key to post-traumatic stress lies in brain chemistry, scientists find. *New York Times*, pp. B5, B9.

Graham, M. G. (1990). *The expanding role of the rehabilitation specialist as an expert witness*. Unpublished manuscript.

Grothaus, R. S. (1985). Abuse of women with disabilities. In S. E. Browne, D. Connors & N. Stern (Eds.), *With the power of each breath: A disabled women's anthology* (pp. 124-130). Pittsburgh: Cleis Press.

Gueron, J. M. (1989). Work programs for welfare recipients. In S. L. Harlan & R. J. Steinberg (Eds.), *Job training for women* (pp. 365-388). Philadelphia: Temple University press.

Gundle, R. (1986). Civil liability for police failure to arrest: Nearing v. Weaver. *Women's Rights Law Reporter, 9*(3,4), 259-265.

Hall, D. (1990, Winter). Concerns of differently abled women. *NCADV Voice*, p. 5.

Harlan, S. L. (1989). Welfare, workfare, and training. In S. L. Harlan & R. J. Steinberg (Eds.), *Job training for women* (pp. 359-364). Philadelphia: Temple University Press.

Harlan, S. L. & Steinberg, R. J. (1989). Job training for women: The problem in a policy context. In S. L. Harlan & R. J. Steinberg (Eds.), *Job training for women* (pp. 3-50).

Heilbrun, C. G. (1988). *Writing a woman's life*. New York: W. W. Norton & Company.

Herrenkohl, E. C., Herrenkohl, R. C., & Toedter, L. J. (1983). Intergenerational transmission of abuse. In D. Finkelhor, R. J. Gelles, G. T. Hotaling, & M. A. Straus (Eds.), *The dark side of families: Current family violence research* (pp. 305-316). Beverly Hills: Sage Publications.

Hine, D. C. (1989, Summer). Rape and the inner lives of black women in the middle west: Preliminary thoughts on the culture of dissemblance. *Sings: Journal of Women in Culture and Society, 14*(4), 912-920.

Hobson, B. M. (1987). *Uneasy virtue: The politics of prostitution and the American reform tradition.* New York: Basic Books.

How many wars can the U.S. fight? (1991, March 4). *Time Magazine,* pp. 38-39.

Hunter, S. K., & Reed, K. C. (Speakers). (1990, July). *Taking the side of bought and sold rape* (Cassette Recording). Washington, DC: National Coalition Against Sexual Assault.

Ibrahim, F. A., & Herr, E. L. (1987). Battered women: A developmental life-career counseling perspective. *Journal of Counseling and Development, 65,* 244-248.

Institute for the Study of Sexual Assault. (1983-1987). *Civil sexual assault cases: Judgments and settlements.* San Francisco: Author.

Johnson, B. (1989, February 13). A love betrayed, a brief life lost. *People Magazine,* p. 84.

Johnson, M. (1987). CABE and strippers: A delicate union. In L. Bell (Ed.), *Good girls, bad girls: Feminists and sex trade workers face to face* (pp. 109-112). Seattle: The Seal Press.

Judicial Council Advisory Committee On Gender Bias in the Courts (1990). *Achieving equal justice for women and men in the courts.* San Francisco: Administrative Office of the Courts.

Karp, L., & Karp, C. L. (1989). *Domestic torts: Family violence, conflict and sexual abuse.* New York: Shepard's/McGraw Hill, Inc.

Kennedy, R. D. (1983). *California expert witness guide.* Berkeley: CEB Publications.

Kilpatrick, D. G., Veronen, L. J., & Best, C. L. (1985). Factors predicting psychological distress among rape victims. In C. R. Figley (Ed.), *Trauma and its wake: The study and treatment of post-traumatic stress disorder* (pp. 113-141). New York: Brunner/Mazel.

Klepfisz, I. (1990). *Dreams of an insomniac: Jewish feminist essays, speeches and diatribes.* Portland, OR: Eighth Mountain Press.

Koop, C. E. (1990, Spring). Address to the Pan American Health Organization on May 22, 1989. *Newsline: Office of Criminal Justice Planning Quarterly Newsletter, 5*(1), 1.

Koss, M. P. (1988). Hidden rape: Sexual aggression and victimization in a national sample of students in higher education. In A. W. Burgess (Ed.), *Rape and sexual assault II* (pp. 3-26). New York: Garland Publishing.

Kuhn, T. S. (1970). *The structure of scientific revolutions.* Chicago: University of Chicago Press.

Lamoreauz, D. (Ed.). (1990, August). *ADA compliance guide.* Washington, DC: Thompson Publishing Group.

Largen, M. A. (1988). *Rape-law reform: An analysis. In A. W. Burgess (Ed.), Rape and sexual assault II* (pp. 271-290). New York: Garland Publishing.

Lasky, H. (1988). *Guidelines for handling psychiatric issues in workers' compensation cases.* Rancho Palos Verdes, CA: Lexcom Enterprises.

Ledray, L. E. (1988). Responding to the needs of rape victims: Research findings. In A. W. Burgess (Ed.), *Rape and sexual assault II* (pp. 169-192). New York: Garland Publishing.

Leonoesio, M. V. (1989). Recent trends in women's use of time and their implications for assessing the replacement cost of household services. *Journal of Forensic Economics, 1*(2), 47-53.

Liss, M. (1980). *Prostitution in perspective: A comparison of prostitutes and other working women.* Unpublished doctoral dissertation, Northern Illinois University, DeKalb.

Long-Scott, E. (1990, July). Link up the struggles for real social justice. *Economic Justice Speakout, 4*(3), 25.

Louise, M. (1980, May). *Leaving the clerical track: A feminist analysis.* Unpublished master's thesis, Vermont College (formerly Goddard College), Plainfield.

Lukas, J. (1990, August). The stirrings of history: A new world rises from the ruins of empire. *Atlantic Monthly,* p. 41.

MacKinnon, C. (1987). *Feminism unmodified: Discourses on life and law.* Cambridge, MA: Harvard University Press.

Magrowski, J. F. (1991, March). Future vocational expert testimony on hedonics (pp. 72-78). *Monograph #1: The vocational expert's testimony.* Topeka, KS: American Board of Vocational Experts.

Major federal legislation to protect women from violence. (1991, February-April). *Heartened: Newsletter of the Central Texas Formerly Battered Women's Task Force,* p. 10.

Massaro, T. M. (1985). The rape trauma syndrome issue and its implications for expert psychological testimony. *Minnesota Law Review, 69,* 395.

Matthaei, J. A. (1982). *An economic history of women in America: Women's work, the sexual division of labor and the development of capitalism.* New York: Shocken Books.

May, R. (1983). *The discovery of being: Writings in existential psychology.* New York: W. W. Norton & Company.

McLanahan, S. S., Sorensen, A., & Watson, D. (1989). Sex differences in poverty, 1950-1980. *Signs: A Journal of Women in Culture and Society, 15*(1), 102-121.

McNulty, F. (1980). *The burning bed.* New York: Avon Books.

Meiselman, K. C. (1984). *Incest: A psychological study of causes and effects with treatment recommendations.* San Francisco: Josey-Bass Publishers.

Metcalf, R. E. (1990a). *Determining rehabilitation economic damages: A training supplement.* San Diego: The San Diego Institute.

Miller, A. (1981). *The drama of the gifted child.* New York: Basic Books.

Miller, A. (1984a). *For your own good: Hidden cruelty in child-rearing and the roots of violence.* New York: Farrar, Straus, Giroux.

Miller, A. (1984b). *Thou shalt not be aware: Society's betrayal of the child.* New York: New American Library.

Miller, A. (1986). *Pictures of a childhood.* New York: Farrar, Straus, Giroux.

Miller, A. (1988). *The untouched day: Tracing childhood trauma in creativity and destructiveness.* New York: Doubleday.

Miller, J. (1989). Displaced homemakers in the employment and training system. In S. L. Harlan & R. J. Steinberg (Eds.), *Job training for women* (pp. 143-165). Philadelphia: Temple University Press.

Millett, K. (1970). *Sexual politics.* New York: Avon.

Millett, K. (1976). *The prostitution papers.* New York: Ballantine Books.

Minnesota Institute of Legal Education. (1990, July). *Premises liability.* Minneapolis: Author.

Minnich, E. K. (1990). *Transforming knowledge.* Philadelphia: Temple University Press.

Minzer, M., Nates, J. H., Kimball, C. D., Axelrod, D. T., & Goldstein, R. P. (1989). *Damages in tort actions.* New York: Matthew Bender.

Morgan, R. (1989). *The demon lover: On the sexuality of terrorism.* New York: W. W. Norton.

Moustakas, C. (1988). *Phenomenology, science, and psychotherapy.* Cape Breton, Canada: Family Life Institute, University College of Cape Breton.

Mudrick, N. R. (1988). Disabled women and public policies for income support. In M. Fine & A. Asch (Eds.), *Women with disabilities: Essays in psychology, culture and politics* (pp. 245-268). Philadelphia: Temple University Press.

Murphy, P. A. (1987). *Searching for spring.* Tallahassee, FL: The Naiad Press.

Murphy, P. A. (1988a). Abuse: A blight on our success. In W. Wood & L. Hatton (Eds.), *Triumph over darkness: Understanding and healing the trauma of childhood sexual abuse* (pp. 32-37). Hillsboro, OR: Beyond Words Publishing, Inc.

Murphy, P. A. (1988b). *We walk the back of the tiger.* Tallahassee, FL: The Naiad Press.

Murphy, P. A. (1992). Taking an abuse history in the initial evaluation. *NARPPS Journal & News* 7(5), 187-191.

Myers, J. E. B. (1991, January). Cross-examination of expert witnesses regarding a personal history of victimization. *Violence Update*, p. 9.

National Association of Business Economists. (1988). *Salary characteristics*. Cleveland, OH: Author.

National Association of Rehabilitation Professionals in the Private Sector (NARPPS) (1989/1990). *National directory of rehabilitation professionals, vocational/medical facilities/products and devices.* Brookline, MA: Author.

National Coalition Against Domestic Violence. (1990, August). *Resolution to support the National Pro Bono Vocational Rehabilitation Movement offered by the members of the National Association of Rehabiltiation Professionals in the Private Sector (NARPPS).* Amherst, MA: Author.

National Coalition Against Sexual Assault. (1990a, July). *Resolution for NCASA to recognize prostitution as violence against women.* Membership meeting conducted at the meeting of the National Coalition Against Sexual Assault, Denver, Colorado.

National Coalition Against Sexual Assault. (1990b, July). *Resolution for support for sex trade workers.* Membership meeting conducted at the meeting of the National Coalition Against Sexual Assault, Denver, Colorado.

Neland, V. (undated). *CPA Handbook.* (Available from Council for Prostitution Alternatives, 710 S. E. Grand Avenue, #8, Portland, Oregon.)

Nevada Revised Statutes, Annotated (4) (1991). 125.155 (8).

Parson, E. R. (1985). Ethnicity and traumatic stress: The intersecting point in psychotherapy. In C. R. Figley (Ed.), *Trauma and its wake: The study and treatment of posttraumatic stress disorder* (pp. 314-335). New York: Brunner/Mazel.

Pawel, E. (1984). *The nightmare of reason: A life of Franz.* New York: Vintage Books.

Pearce, D. (1978, February). The feminization of poverty: Women, work and welfare. *Urban and Social Change Review, 11,* 28-36.

Pitt, D. E. (1989a, December 8). Canada unnerved by slayings of 14. *New York Times,* p. 9.

Pitt, D. E. (1989b, December 9). Suicide note faulting women found on body of Montreal gunman. *New York Times,* p. 6.

Private Rehabilitation Suppliers of Georgia Ethics and Standards Committee. (1989, July). *Ethical issues in private sector rehabilitation: Case summaries for discussion.* Athens, GA: P Elliott & Fitzpatrick.

Reis, D. (1991, Winter). Capital update. *National Business Woman,* p. 4.

Rhode, D. L. (1990). Gender equality and employment policy. In S. E. Rix (Ed.), *The American woman: 1990-91* (pp. 170-200). New York: W. W. Norton & Company.

Rix, S. E. (Ed.). (1990). *The American woman 1990-1991.* New York: W. W. Norton & Company.

Rush, F. (1980). *The best kept secret: Sexual abuse of children.* New York: McGraw-Hill.

Russell, D. E. H. (1984). *Sexual exploitation: Rape, child sexual abuse, and workplace harassment.* Beverly Hills: Sage Publications.

Russell, D. E. H. (1986). *The secret trauma: Incest in the lives of girls and women.* New York: Basic Books.

Russell, D. E. H. (1988). *Pornography and rape: A causal model.* Political Psychology, 9(1), 41-73.

Russell, D. E. H. (1990a, July). *From witches to bitches: Sexual terrorism against women.* Presented at the meeting of the National Coalition Against Domestic Violence, Denver, CO.

Russell, D. E. H. (1990b). *Rape in marriage.* Bloomington, IN: Indiana University Press.

Ryan, J. (1990). Legalized prostitution in Nevada. In D. Gamache (Ed.), *A facilitator's guide to prostitution: A matter of violence against women* (pp. 16-20). Minneapolis: WHISPER.

Sanders, J. (1988). *Staying poor: How the job training partnership act fails women.* Metuchen, NJ: Scarecrow Press.

Saxton, M., & Howe, F. (1987). Introduction. In M. Saxton & F. Howe (Eds.), *With wings: An anthology of literature by and about women with disabilities* (pp. xi-xv). New York: The Feminist Press.

Saydah, A. (1990, Fall). Research in review: The latest on family intervention. *Headlines: The Brain Injury Magazine*, p. 12.

Schechter, S. (1982). *Women and male violence: The visions and struggles of the battered women's movement.* Boston: South End Press.

Schmidt, M. J., Crimando, W., & Riggar, T. F. (1990). *Sexual harassment in the workplace: A trainer's guide.* Athens, GA: Elliott & Fitzpatrick.

Sherman, R. (1990, October). *The marital standard of living: Trial, statement of decision and appeal.* Berkeley: CEB Publications.

Silbert, M. H. (1988). Compounding factors in the rape of street prostitutes. In A. W. Burgess (Ed.), *Rape and sexual assault II* (pp. 75-90). New York: Garland Publishing.

Silbert, M. H., & Pines, A. M. (1982). Victimization of street prostitutes. *Victimology: An International Journal, 7*(1-4), 122-133.

Smith, S. V. (1988, September 1). Hedonic damages in wrongful death cases. *ABA Journal, 74*, 70.

Springer, C. E., Agosti, D. A., Derby, J., Ford, J., England, K., Landreth, K., McGroarty, J. S., Melton, R., Piscevich, M., White, E. W., & Young, L. A. (1987). *Justice for women: First report of the Nevada Supreme Court Task force on gender bias in the courts.* Carson City: Supreme Court of Nevada.

Stout, K. D. (1991, February). Intimate femicide: A national demographic overview. *Violence Update*, p. 3.

Strong, T. (1988). I give thanks for the sky. In E. Bass & L. Davis (Eds.), *The courage to heal: A guide for women survivors of child sexual abuse* (pp. 84-85). New York: Harper & Row.

Summitt, R. (1983). The child abuse accommodation syndrome. *Child Abuse and Neglect*, p. 177.

Symanski, R. (1974, September). Prostitution in Nevada. *Annals of the Association of American Geographers, 64*(2), 357-377.

Theodoulou, M. S. (1990). *Using general semantics to heal the invisible scars from verbal-emotional abuse (psychological maltreatment).* Unpublished doctoral dissertation, The Union Institute, Cincinnati, OH.

Thompson Publishing Group. (1990). *ADA compliance guide.* Salisbury, MD: Author.

Trapasso, C. (1991, March). Market update. *California Worker's Compensation Enquirer*, p. 26.

Trimble, M. R. (1985). Post-traumatic stress disorder: History of a concept. In C. R. Figley (Ed.), *Trauma and its wake: The study and treatment of post-traumatic stress disorder* (p. 5-15). New York: Brunner/Mazel.

United States Department of Commerce. (1975). *Statistical abstracts.* Bureau of the Census.

United States Department of Labor, Bureau of Labor Statistics (1972-1973). *Occupational outlook handbook.* Indianapolis, IN: JIST Works, Inc.

United States Department of Labor, Bureau of Labor Statistics (1977-1978). *Occupational outlook handbook.* Indianapolis, IN: JIST Works, Inc.

United States Department of Labor, Bureau of Labor Statistics (1990-1991). *Occupational outlook handbook.* Indianapolis, IN: JIST Works, Inc.

University of Nevada, General Catalog. (1990-1991). Reno, NV: University of Nevada.

Wages for housework: Sample letter to congress (1990, Fall). *NWSAction 3*(3), 21-22

Walker, L. E. (1979). *The battered woman.* New York: Perennial Library.

Walker, L. E. (1989). *Terrifying love: Why battered women kill and how society responds.* New York: Harper & Row.

Waring, M. (1988). *If women counted: A new feminist economics.* San Francisco: Harper & Row.

Watson, C. G., Juba, M. P., Manifold, V., Kucala, T., & Anderson, P. E. D. (1991, March). The PTSD interview: Rationale, description, reliability, and concurrent validity of a DSM-III-based technique. *Journal of Clinical Psychology, 47*(2), 188.

Weed, R. O., & Field, T. F. (1986, Summer). The differences and similarities between public & private sector vocational rehabilitation: A literature review. *Journal of Applied Rehabilitation Counseling 17*(2), 11-14.

Wiegan, S. (1990, October 7). 43 women slain–San Diego cops linked. *The Sacramento Bee*, p. A-15.

Weitzman, L. J. (1985). *The divorce revolution: The unexpected social and economic consequences for women and children in America*. New York: The Free Press.

WHISPER (Producer) (1990). *Prostitution: A matter of violence against women* (Videotape). Minneapolis: WHISPER, Inc.

Williams, B. L. (1989, December 7). Killing us twice: Lies of our times. *San Francisco Chronicle*, p. 16.

Williams, J. M. (1990, November). Industrial rehabilitation: An expanding market for the vocational experts. *The Vocational Expert*, 7(4), 4-6.

Wilson, J. P., Smith, W. K., & Johnson, S. K. (1985). A comparative analysis of PTSD among various survivor groups. In C. R. Figley (Ed.), *Trauma and its wake: The study and treatment of post-traumatic stress disorder* (pp. 142-172). New York: Brunner/Mazel.

Woods, L. (1981). Litigation on the behalf of battered women. *Women's Rights Law Reporter, 7*, 39.

Yegidis, B. L. (1989). *Abuse risk inventory for women manual*. Palo Alto, CA: Consulting Psychologist Press.

appendix one

---

about the study

This book is based on the systematic coding of 496 closed workers' compensation cases for abuse factors; heuristic and phenomenological interviews with eight women survivors of rape, battering, and incest; a decade of clinical vocational rehabilitation counseling experience in workers' compensation systems with survivors of abuse; dissolution of marriage cases; a counseling group for formerly battered women; career and life planning counseling sessions; a decade of experience as an employer of women clerical and professional workers; a literature review of Post-traumatic Stress Disorder (PTSD) categories: Battered Woman Syndrome (BWS), Rape Trauma Syndrome (RTS), and Child Abuse Accommodation Syndrome (CAAS); a literature review of current methods for determining lost earning capacity for survivors of injuries in civil law suits; a literature review of civil sexual assault cases resulting in damage awards; a literature review of prostitution; and a literature review of women's work patterns. I would like to write that I also reviewed literature regarding women, work, and abuse, but the two articles available hardly qualify as a literature review (Bowen, 1982; Ibrahim & Herr, 1987).

workers' compensation cases analysis

The 496 closed workers' compensation cases were coded by me, for abuse factors, onto Scantron forms for computer analysis. A random sample of cases were coded to insure inter-rater reliability by a graduate student in counseling.

The cases were drawn from my private practice as a vocational rehabilitation counselor providing vocational rehabilitation services to industrially injured workers from 1979 to 1989 in the Los Angeles area. Cases were referred from private workers' compensation insurance carriers and state workers' compensation systems in California and Nevada. Attorneys representing both insurance carriers and injured workers have considerable influence over the choice of a vocational rehabilitation counselor, and therefore they should also be considered referral sources even though it is the insurance carrier who pays for the provision of services. I personally handled more than 95% of the cases, with the remaining 5% handled by my small counseling staff under my supervision.

Services were provided to 160 women and 336 men, a ratio of 32.2% women to 67.7% men. This is 3.4% higher than the 1989 statistics for female participation in the California workers' compensation system according to data compiled by the California Workers' Compensation Institute (1990). It is not clear why this should be so, but perhaps my reputation for willingness to work with female injured workers influenced my referral sources and thus led to a higher rate of female participation.

Twelve of the women in my study were African-American, two were Asian, 36 were of Hispanic origin, 105 were Caucasian, and three fell into the category of *other*. (Two were not coded.)

Two women were between the ages of 15 to 20 years; 37 were between 21 to 30 years; 49 were between 31 to 40 years; 39 were between 41 to 50 years; and 20 were between 51 to 80 years. (Eight were not coded.)

Forty-three of the 160 women in my caseload received limited services (e.g., such as eligibility determination) only. Consequently, very little data were available in the case files for these women. One hundred and seventeen women received services beyond eligibility determination and, as a result, more data could be gleaned from the case files.

Of the 117 case files analyzed, 8.54% of women had suffered on-the-job abuse injuries, including rape/sexual assault (2); physical assault (4); and emotional abuse (4).

Abuse outside of the waged labor market was experienced by 26.5% of the women, including wife battering (17); rape/sexual assault (1); marital rape (1); parental (elder) abuse (2); childhood battering (5); childhood sexual abuse (10). Some women had experienced multiple abuse.

The data are remarkable when one considers that survivors are at the very real risk of having benefits reduced or of losing benefits entirely as a result of disclosing abuse histories. In workers' compensation systems, compensable injuries must meet the test of having arisen out of a work injury.

The number of rape/sexual assault cases is probably small because on-the-job sexual assaults are handled under employment law as sex discrimination, rather than under workers' compensation law. The number of off-the-job rapes is probably small because at that time, I, in my role as a vocational rehabilitation counselor, was not comfortable asking clients for their rape histories. Therefore, I was also not available as the open, committed listener for rape survivors. Family violence issues (e.g., incest, child and wife battering) were more accessible to me and my clients, since family dynamics are considered to be within a vocational rehabilitation counselor's purview if they impinge on the rehabilitation process.

The data, of course, do not lend themselves to generalization, but do suggest that vocational rehabilitation counselors would be well served to educate themselves regarding the realities of abuse dynamics and their interaction with the experience of industrial injury in workers' compensation vocational rehabilitation processes.

the heuristic and phenomenological interviews

A heuristic interview is one in which the researcher and the co-researcher share the experience to be explored in the interview. As a survivor of the incest trauma, acquaintance rape, attempted stranger rape, and inducement to prostitution, I was able to extend an invitation to conversation based on shared knowledge and experience.

Co-researchers who were survivors of wife battering and child battering were interviewed phenomenologically. That is, I acknowledged my lack of personal experience and attempted to be genuinely present, committed, and open to the co-researcher (Moustakas, 1988).

In both cases, the co-researchers were asked the following questions: What is your experience of abuse? What has been your recovery process? What has been the impact of your abuse experience and recovery process on your work life?

Eight women were interviewed, producing 509 pages of transcript based on interviews ranging from one and one-half hours to more than four hours. The interviews were audiotaped and the audio tapes and the transcripts were reviewed intensively resulting in the stories placed in front of each chapter. Interview questions were eliminated for the sake of brevity, and also to allow the co-researchers' voices to be heard in the most powerful way.

The co-researchers were not part of my workers' compensation caseload, nor were they ever clients of mine in any setting. The co-researchers were located at the Summer 1990 national conventions of the National Coalition Against Sexual Assault in Denver, Colorado, and the National Coalition Against Domestic Violence in Amherst, Massachusetts, as well as through my contacts with workers in rape crisis centers and battered women shelters. One woman was referred from a college.

The exact ethnic and racial configuration of the eight co-researchers is protected in order to preserve confidentiality. The women ranged in age from 28 to 47 years, and between them they had experienced acquaintance rape (1); marital rape (3); stranger rape (1); wife battering (3); childhood sexual abuse (4); childhood battering (4). This is a total of 16 easily identifiable abuse experiences between eight women, some of which was continuous over a period of months, or even years.

appendix two

further research suggestions

Men, work, and abuse: Men did show up as abused in my analysis of my closed workers' compensation cases. There were seven men with histories of childhood battering and four men with childhood sexual abuse histories. It is my opinion that these figures are low and do not represent actual abuse rates. I do believe that abuse, for men, presents vocational dysfunction as well as for women, but since the work lives of men and women are so different, it is not possible for me to address these complexities in one book.

Prostitution survivors and post-traumatic stress disorder: An examination of post-traumatic stress disorder in the prostitution survivor population as compared to other populations (e.g., combat veterans) and (nonprostituted women) rape survivors would provide badly needed data. As long as prostitution is not perceived as violence against women, we will have little knowledge of the psychological and/or physical injuries experienced by this class of women.

The vulnerable years: An exploration of the vocational outcomes of women raped during the vulnerable years (13-26) as compared to the young men who have raped them would be instructive. The anecdotal evidence from the popular press on campus rape seems to indicate that the women drop out of school or delay their educations while their rapists complete college and go on to lucrative careers.

Theories of vocational choice: How is vocational identity developed for women? Sustained? Nurtured? Can vocational identity be healed or regained after traumatic abuse? Do women choose occupations based on safety factors rather than interest, income, or job satisfaction? Is it reasonable to expect newly divorced homemakers to have fully developed work or vocational identities? How does legalized prostitution as a societal norm affect the career choices of young women who live in such environments?

Hedonic damage awards based on loss of occupations: Just the formulation of proper research questions is challenging. Should there be a statistical analysis of dissolution of marriage cases by vocational outcomes? What about looking at domestic violence cases by vocational outcomes? Or the costs of implementing mandatory arrest in domestic violence cases per life saved? What about analyzing rape cases by vocational outcomes? Childhood battering and sexual abuse by vocational outcomes?

Shelters for formerly battered women and their children, rape crisis centers, and agencies serving prostitution survivors: These agencies should be studied for their vocational rehabilitative functions through the provision of volunteer and staff positions drawn from survivors. What are the vocational outcomes after volunteers and staff, who are also survivors, leave the agency?

appendix three

---

the making the connections project

The Making The Connections Project is an Affiliate Project of The Union Institute Center For Women in Washington, DC.

The Project is an outgrowth of a partnership between the rehabilitation communities and the anti-abuse communities. This partnership was first acknowledged on August 4, 1990 when the National Coalitation Against Domestic Violence passed a resolution (see Appendix 6) at their national convention accepting the pro bono services of the members of the National Association of Rehabilitation Professionals in the Private Sector.

The goal of the Affiliate Project is to engage the anti-abuse communities and the rehabilitation communities in the creation of a dynamic and synergistic partnership which will serve to:

1. Acknowledge the damage caused by abuse to women's vocational aspirations, development, and achievements.

2. Evolve vocational rehabilitation practice and theory which will enable women abuse survivors to engage in suitable productive activities in the waged or unwaged work arenas.

The Project now publishes the quarterly *Vocational Rehabilitation & Abuse Newsletter,* and *The Working Papers.*

The first paper, "Taking an Abuse History in the Initial Evaluation", was published by the *NARPPS Journal & News* in October 1992. This paper is a how-to document to be used by rehabilitationists and anti-abuse workers. The paper is now available as a reprint from the Project.

The Project also sponsors The Making The Connections Meetings and Seminars. The first in this series was held on the campus of St. Cloud State University and in the community of St. Cloud, Minnesota in April 1992. The next in the series will be held in Seattle, Washington in 1993.

For more information about the Project and its activities, contact: The Making The Connections Project, The Union Institute Center For Women, 1731 Connecticut Avenue, NW, Suite 300, Washington, DC 20009-1146. The telephone number is (202) 667-1313.

appendix four

---

primary care vocational service delivery standards

Preamble: NARPPS members recognize the uniqueness of providing Private Sector Rehabilitation Services under various federal and state laws and insurance coverages, however; there remain broad service standards that should be applied regardless of this uniqueness. Primary Care Vocational Rehabilitation Services are those vocational services provided directly to a client, the goal of which is to return a client to suitable gainful employment. The following standards are criteria against which Primary Care Vocational Rehabilitation Services can be measured. NARPPS members will adhere to these Service Standards unless such adherence is contraindicated by laws, regulations, or client needs:

A. Referral

There are certain standards that should be met before a client is accepted for vocational service. The following minimal information should accompany a referral for service:

Reprinted with permission from Standards and Ethics. *NARPPS 1989/1990 National Directory of Rehabilitation Professionals, Vocational/Medical Facilities, Products and Services*, pp. 19-26. Brookline, MA.

1. Client identifying data
2. All pertinent medical and medically related data
3. Purpose of referral
4. Referrer special instructions for service, if any

Rehabilitation Practitioners may also refer to outside vendors or other Practitioners. The same minimal information should be provided with special emphasis given to purpose of referral and special requests for service.

B. Vocational Evaluation

The first step in the vocational rehabilitation process is evaluation. Depending on the purpose of the referral, the Rehabilitation Practitioner may emphasize various elements of the evaluation; however, the following points should be addressed in any written evaluation:

1. Statement of purpose for, and conditions under which, evaluation occurred
2. Brief summary of referral records
3. Client's medical status including history of current injury/illness, description of functional limitations and abilities, previous significant medical history, current medical care including identification of treating physician(s)
4. Schedule of Physician/Therapist appointments pending
5. Client's vocational history including skills, intelligence, academic achievement, primary aptitudes, and transferable skills
6. Client's education and specialized training, whether formal or informal
7. Client's interest(s), reading skills, intelligence, academic achievement, primary aptitudes, and transferable skills
8. Summary of data with emphasis on client's assets and limitations, with recommendations to facilitate the purpose of the referral

C. Plan Development

Rehabilitation Practitioners may write a myriad of vocational plans depending upon coverage, jurisdiction, purposes of referral, etc. However, NARPPS members recognize that there are certain plan standards that should be met whenever a written plan is developed.

1. The client should be an active participant within his/her physical/mental capacity in the plan development
2. When a plan is written, all interested parties should agree before its implementation
3. The plan should be signed by the client and/or his/her representative and the Rehabilitation Practitioner
4. The plan should identify clearly stated goal(s) with action(s) directed towards achieving this goal(s)
5. The plan should identify all parties' responsibilities, the action steps for which they are responsible (including fiscal), and the time frames for completion
6. A rationale for the plan, integrating the elements of the evaluation, should be included
7. The criteria for completion, termination, or suspension should be clearly delineated

D. Job Development and Placement

Job development is the activity by which a client begins the placement process. Job placement is the goal of job development. Taken together, their goal is finding and placing a client into suitable, gainful employment. The following standards should be met by Rehabilitation Practitioners who provide job development and placement services:

1. Confirmation of the client's job readiness and general readiness for employment

2. Obtain client agreement to actively participate in the job seeking process
3. Assure the presence of client job seeking and job holding skills
4. Identify the client's transferable skills
5. Document appropriateness of prospective jobs as they relate to client skills and limitation
6. Inform prospective employers of client skills and limitations
7. Assist employer in complying with various requirements for immigration, job tax credits, second injury funds, etc.
8. Monitor client job adjustment and progress as needed to insure appropriate work adjustment.

Rehabilitation Practitioners recognize that one of the surest methods of obtaining both vocational training and a successful job placement is through the use of an on-the-job training program. The following requirements should be met when providing an on-the-job training service:

1. Written agreement outlining time frames and responsibilities of all parties
2. Identification of skills to be learned
3. Confirmation that client will be treated as an "employee" with the same benefits as all other employees
4. Affirmation that client will perform as a reliable employee without expecting undue privileges
5. Terms of payment to employer
6. Terms of compensation to the client
7. Conditions under which agreement is to be completed and/or terminated including any agreement by employer to hire client.

E. Report Writing and Recordkeeping

Rehabilitation Practitioners understand that reporting requirements differ between referral sources and jurisdictions. Some referral sources demand frequent written reports while others require less frequency. Therefore, the frequency of reporting to the referral source should be determined at referral and compliance should be consistent with that determination.

Regardless of reporting frequency, there are certain recordkeeping standards to which adherence is required. The following records, when they exist, should be in the file at all times:

1. Written evaluation
2. Written plan
3. Written closure report
4. Written agreements such as on-the-job training, release of client records, responsibilities, etc.
5. Medical/psychological reports
6. Correspondence between interested parties
7. Regulatory orders affecting or related to the client

Client records should be secured to insure confidentiality and should not be disclosed without client authorization or legal requirement. Records should be maintained for the number of years after closure that is consistent with jurisdictional requirements. After that time, they should be destroyed in a manner assuring preservation of confidentiality.

F. Closure

Rehabilitation Practitioners recognize that services may terminate at any point in the vocational rehabilitation process. There are several situations that may result in either a successful or unsuccessful resolution to rehabilitation. At least one of the following situations should exist before closing a file:

1. Rehabilitation goals have been achieved
2. Further services will most probably not result in client's improvement
3. Services have been declined by client or authorized representative

4. Client is no longer available for services
5. Administrative terminations including case settlement, policy limits exhausted, regulatory directives, third party payor termination, etc.

Once any of the above situations has occurred, the Rehabilitation Practitioner should document the justification for rehabilitation closure as follows:

1. Document follow-up activities supporting the achievement of goals
2. Document results of evaluation supporting the improbability of client improvement
3. Document lack of client interest, declination, or non-availability
4. Document the unavailability of rehabilitation funding
5. Document administrative terminations

Upon closure, if the Rehabilitation Professional is aware of client needs which may be met by community resources/similar benefits, they should refer the client to these resources.

G. Dispute Resolution

NARPPS members recognize that there will be occasions when disputes occur between parties involved in the vocational rehabilitation process. It is the Rehabilitation Practitioner's responsibility to assist in resolving these disputes as quickly as possible. The following services may be provided by the Rehabilitation Practitioner in resolving these disputes:

1. Written definition of the dispute
2. Written definition of the positions taken by each of the interested parties in the dispute
3. Informal attempt at dispute resolution

4. Formal attempt, including conferences, administrative hearings and other regulatory assistance
5. Written statement of resolution outlining responsibilities of all interested parties

appendix five

---

areas of expertise needed by vocational experts in abuse cases*

The vocational expert is a professional who possesses the following areas of expertise related to assessment, employability and wage loss analysis, labor market information, and rehabilitation planning of vocational issues of the injured individual:

1. Knowledge of the field of vocational rehabilitation including federal and state laws and regulations of pertinent programs;
2. Knowledge of vocational, educational, and psychological assessment procedures, including tests, work samples, situational evaluations used in the assessment of vocational potential;
3. Knowledge of and ability to utilize standard references covering issues of workforce, labor markets, occupations, wage data resources;
4. Knowledge of and ability to determine transferability of skills and to utilize this analysis in determining loss of vocational functioning as the result of injury or trauma;

---

*Partially adapted from G. Michael Graham's (1990) seminar materials on *The Expanding Role of the Rehabilitation Specialist As Expert Witness.*

5. Knowledge of and ability to analyze jobs for both previous and possible future employment as they exist in the local economy;

6. Ability to determine the potential for probable future employment of the injured worker's transferable skills and capacity to work and the ability to calculate a loss of access to particular jobs that exist in a local economy as the result of the injury's disabling effects;

7. Knowledge of wage earnings data for jobs that exist in the economy. Ability to calculate a wage loss based upon the injured worker's loss of access to employment in that economy. The ability to calculate the loss of power to earn money as a result of injury and the ability to provide employment and earning data for the purpose of calculating the loss of future earnings that is fair and defensible;

8. Knowledge of and ability with procedures, processes, and resources for rehabilitation planning and/or training relative to the physical and/or psychological needs of the injured worker including clinical interviewing skills, functional assessment procedures, capacity evaluation, planning for services such as medical treatment, job analysis workups, and job placement;

9. Ability to present vocational data in depositions and judicial hearings;

10. Ability to serve as a consultant to other professionals involved in the total rehabilitation process of the injured worker;

11. Ability to assist attorneys in the development of case presentation strategy including the development of depositional and trial questions of opposing experts;

12. Ability to present written reports of findings and opinions;

13. Knowledge of rape shield law provisions and the ability to discuss the implications of obtaining abuse history experience(s) prior to the assault in question with plaintiff's attorney;

14. Knowledge of and ability to explain PTSD and its subcategories; Rape Trauma Syndrome, Battered Women Syndrome, and Child Abuse Accommodation Syndrome;

15. Knowledge of and ability to use such assessment instruments as the PTSD-1 Interview or The Abuse Assessment Inventory;

16. Knowledge of the common physical injuries of abuse survivors and their impact on vocational functioning;

17. Knowledge of and ability to explain prostitution as the center of the rape paradigm concept particularly in cases involving prostitution survivors and women and children used in pornography and/or prostitution;

18. Knowledge of the "vulnerable years" for rape including marital rape and extortion or inducement to prostitution (13-26) and the impact of rape on vocational identity formation;

19. Knowledge of and ability to explain work patterns by gender, race, age, marital status, including educational attainment levels, labor market access, and wage differentials;

20. Knowledge of women's unwaged work lives which may include child care, elder care, and housework and the impact of injury on both the waged and unwaged aspects of a woman's worklife;

21. Knowledge of the inappropriateness of confusing or subsuming a woman's work identity with or under her social role as wife and/or mother;

22. Knowledge of the importance of child care considerations in all vocational planning assessments and efforts for injured workers with children;

23. Knowledge of the value of domestic tort law which creates a framework for a lost earning capacity analysis based on the impact of domestic violence;

24. Knowledge of the hedonic value of professions/ occupations above and beyond the value of lost earnings;

25. Knowledge of how to respond to questions about your own possible abuse history which might disqualify you as an expert witness because of "bias."

appendix six

---

resolution for the national coalition against domestic violence*

Resolution for the National Coalition Against Domestic Violence (NCADV) to support the national pro bono vocational rehabilitation movement offered by the members of the National Association of Rehabilitation Professionals in the Private Sector (NARPPS). (Passed by the NCADV at the Annual Membership Meeting on August 4, 1990 at the University of Massachusetts at Amherst.)

WHEREAS the NCADV is dedicated to the empowerment of battered women;
WHEREAS to economic oppression of battered women is central to the maintenance of violence against women;
WHEREAS the shelter movement faces financial jeopardy as an ongoing reality;
WHEREAS the 1988 Women's Action Alliance report on the Job Training and Partnership Act (JTPA) indicates that the JTPA is not effective in moving low income women out of poverty and into economic self-sufficiency;
WHEREAS other federal and state programs such as workfare, GAIN, and JOBS offer self-esteem programs with convicted wife batterers as role models and that these programs do no designate battered women as a special needs group although teen mothers and displaced homemakers are so designated;

Authored by Patricia A. Murphy and presented by Carol Arnett (1990).

WHEREAS AFDC does not serve the needs of battered women and their children;

WHEREAS the no-fault divorce model has proven to be economic disaster for women and their children and women are not using or are unable to use the services of vocational experts in determining appropriate vocational plans which would lead to economic self-sufficiency;

WHEREAS the battered woman's use of the civil courts in order to collect damages to her lost earning capacity as a result of battering has been non-existent or minimal;

WHEREAS vocational rehabilitation programs offered in State Departments of Rehabilitation and in federal and state workers' compensation systems reveal little or no understanding of Battered Women's Syndrome and the needs of battered women;

WHEREAS the efforts of battered women and formerly battered women to move toward economic self-sufficiency despite these obstacles can only be described as heroic;

BE IT THEREFORE RESOLVED that the NCADV accept the services and advocacy of the members of the NARPPS in a spirit of partnership and acknowledgment of the knowledge and expertise of battered women and formerly battered women and the knowledge and expertise of private sector rehabilitation professionals.